'*101 Inclusive and SEN English Lessons* proves yet again that teachers don't have to make teaching complicated in order to be effective; the key is engaging the learners in having fun. Bradley and Brewer's new book should be an essential daily resource for both teachers and TAs working with children with SEND in the inclusive classroom because these are lessons in which every child can join. This book does exactly what it says in the title.'

– Peter Imray, freelance trainer, adviser and writer on special educational needs

'At a time of rapid change of expectations in schools…Kate and Claire offer some simple yet brilliant ideas that are evidence-based and have proven results. They share their knowledge and understanding of how SEN children may interact, communicate and learn. For anyone looking to transform their teaching practice to be more inclusive, this is your ultimate guidebook!'

– Bavaani Nanthabalan, Executive Headteacher, Netley Primary School & Centre for Autism and Robson House PRU

'A great resource which busy teachers will dip into again and again. The authors are experienced teachers and provide a no-nonsense fast track to some fantastic tried and tested ideas. The lesson plans can be adapted to topic and then repeated, which will help build confidence and self-esteem. Activities are differentiated and pre-verbal students accounted for. An excellent book!'

– Adele Devine, special needs teacher at Portesbery School and JKP author

101 Inclusive & SEN English Lessons

101 Inclusive & SEN English Lessons

FUN ACTIVITIES & LESSON PLANS

for Children Aged 3-11

Kate Bradley and Claire Brewer

Jessica Kingsley *Publishers*
London and Philadelphia

First published in 2018
by Jessica Kingsley Publishers
73 Collier Street
London N1 9BE, UK
and
400 Market Street, Suite 400
Philadelphia, PA 19106, USA

www.jkp.com

Library of Congress Cataloging in Publication Data
A CIP catalog record for this book is available from the Library of Congress

British Library Cataloguing in Publication Data
A CIP catalogue record for this book is available from the British Library

ISBN 978 1 78592 365 4
eISBN 978 1 78450 708 4

Printed and bound in Great Britain

Contents

LISTENING

READING

WRITING

Introduction

The feedback that we received from our first book, *101 Inclusive and SEN Maths Lessons: Fun Activities and Lesson Plans for Children Aged 3–11*, was overwhelming. However, it was not surprising, as the idea for writing these books came from the work that we do in supporting staff and families working with children with SEND (special educational needs and disability). We noticed that many children were having a differentiated National Curriculum lesson, rather than an approach which met their specific learning needs, and so we saw a need for this series of books.

A whole range of people bought our first book, and we thank you for purchasing this one. We know that teaching assistants, mainstream teachers, educational psychologists, speech and language therapists, parents and SEND teachers have all been able to use our first book as a tool to support the children who they teach and work with or support.

We believe that inclusive education means children receiving an education that supports their learning and ensures they make progress. For learners with SEND and complex learning needs, the National Curriculum is not always suitable.

The lessons in this book have all been tried and tested in our own classrooms and are inspired by years of experience in working with the most exciting group of children (we believe!). This book is based on the P Level curriculum.[1] We know that the *Rochford Review* has recommended that we move away from reporting on P Levels, but we feel that it offers a clear developmental pathway to understanding where children have come from and where you can take the teaching next.[2]

What needs to be remembered is that the children who you work with are individuals, and so like any planning you may do, think about the child and

---

1   Department for Education & Standards and Testing Agency (2017) *Performance (P Scale) Attainment Targets for Pupils with Special Educational Needs.* London: DfE.
2   Standards and Testing Agency (2016) *Rochford Review: Final Report.* London: DfE.

tweak the activity to suit their needs. The lessons included in this book fall under four main categories:

1. Speaking

2. Listening

3. Reading

4. Writing.

Within each chapter the lessons start at P4 and work up towards P8. Plenaries have been included for each lesson in order to provide an obvious end point for the child. We have included ideas for ways to consolidate learning as, for children with SEN, doing an activity once is unlikely to support their understanding of a concept.

The book also includes a chapter of starters designed to engage children in motivating learning styles from the beginning of each lesson. It is up to you to decide which starters suit which lesson you are teaching, as you may want to meet a range of additional skills in one session.

We are always creative in our teaching, and so these lessons can be adapted for a one to one situation if needed, but we believe that children learn best surrounded by their peers. We have made the lessons playful and they can be adapted to suit the children's interests, as we know that is also how they learn best. Additionally, we like to avoid worksheets and days of desk-based lessons and so have included a range of additional skills that can be met in the lesson. This can support the Individual Education Planning for the child.

We hope that you find this book useful and inspiring; we loved writing and teaching these lessons and seeing the children in our classes being so motivated to learn, and we hope that you will too!

Thanks

Kate and Claire

Follow us on twitter @Kate_Brads and @clairebrewers

What Do We Mean by Additional Skills?

- Kinaesthetic: movement is important to stimulate the child and provide learning experiences that do not revolve around sitting at a table and chair.

- Auditory: being able to develop listening and processing skills in a variety of subjects across the school day will support children to become more attentive in lessons and life.

- Fine motor: these are the skills that involve doing activities on a smaller scale. Developing these skills supports handwriting, dressing and manipulation in the long term.

- Gross motor: these involve the big muscle groups in the body and are large-scale movements. Developing these skills supports trunk control, co-ordination and motor planning.

- Tactile: skin covers the entire body and is the largest sensory system. Having difficulties processing tactile input (such as getting messy) means that the children don't explore and experience the world to its full potential.

- Attention: a child's ability to attain and engage in activities to their full extent needs time and patience. The ability to focus on an individual activity for a longer period of time enables learning to take place. By providing exciting, short activities you can build a child's tolerance to this.

- Communication: with reference to communication, this is about receptive (listening to) and expressive (responding to) language. Language does not have to be speech; this can be in the form of visuals, communication switches and gesture.

- Social communication: this is about the vital skills of sharing time and experience with a partner, turn taking and knowing rules within social situations and games.

Resources

This is not an exhaustive list, but where possible we have used resources that we find easily in our own classrooms so that life is not made harder for you by having to go out of your way to prepare extra resources for the lessons.

Resources that you will use throughout the book include:

- builder's tray

- choosing board (large firm board with strips of Velcro to attach symbols and pictures)

- laminating sheets and access to a laminator

- water and sand tray

- messy media, for example flour, cornflour and shaving foam/play foam.

- small world characters (toys that children can be imaginative with: animals, dinosaurs, people, etc.)

- toy cars

- toy trains

- whiteboard and pens

- chalk

- felt-tip pens

- pencils

- electronic tablet

- sensory toys (flashing balls, massage cream, hand massagers)

- canvas bag

- tidy up box

- scissors

- teddy bears and dolls

- boxes

- dressing up items

- mirrors

- small magnets and paper clips

- alphabet letters (magnetic, laminated, etc.).

STARTERS

Self-Registration

RESOURCES

Large pieces of paper

Masking tape

Range of coloured felt-tip pens

ACTIVITY

- Set up the activity by using the masking tape to tape the large pieces of paper to the wall/whiteboard around which children will be sitting for the activity. In large upper-case letters write the first letter of each name of the child who will be in the group.

- When the children are sat around the board/wall ask each one to find the letter their name starts with and draw a big line down from that letter to mark themselves as ready to learn.

Teaching note: differentiate this activity by children writing the first letter of their own name.

Say Your Name

RESOURCES

A drum

ACTIVITY

- When the children are sitting in a semicircle adult models singing the song to the tune 'Farmer's in the Den': 'Can you say your name? Can you say your name? (Person's name) (Person's name) can you say your name?'; then adult models banging out the syllables in their name, for example 'Joe-Seph' with two bangs on the drum.

- Go around the circle and all sing the song with the children saying their names, and support them to bang out the syllables in their names using the drum.

Take It in Turns

RESOURCES

Two pocket dice

Photos of the children in the group

Action symbols to fit in the pockets of one of the dice

ACTIVITY

- Set up the activity by placing the photos of the children in one pocket dice and the action symbols in the other pocket dice.

- Choose a child to come to the front of the group using the phrase, for example, 'Lyndsey's turn'.

- The child rolls both dice and then says the child's name and the action to give an instruction to their classmate.

- When each turn has finished, count down and say it is another child's turn, for example '5, 4, 3, 2, 1: Lyndsey's turn has finished – now it's Emma's turn.'

Writing Warm Ups

RESOURCES

Laminated symbols of the warm up activities

Scents/food flavouring

ACTIVITY

- Adult pretends they are doing an exercise class to get ready for writing by being over the top and moving around like a fitness instructor.
- Adult models the following writing warm up activities and the children copy:

  » The caterpillar – bending the index and then the middle finger to walk up the arms.

  » The wall press – find a bit of wall space and do five push ups against the wall.

  » The chair push up – place hands on either side of the body on a chair and push up five times.

  » The prayer push – place hands together in a prayer position and push together ten times.

  » The hand pull – link hands together and try to pull apart ten times.

  » The finger worms – wriggle all ten fingers as fast as you can.

  » The cool down – on the children's right hands place a scent/food flavouring such as peppermint or vanilla.

  » The high five – finish with a high five with the right hand!

Teaching note: the order of these can be mixed up and just doing three or four of them is fine!

Messy Letters

RESOURCES

Builder's tray

Messy media, for example flour and shaving foam

ACTIVITY

- Once the children are sat in a semicircle facing the adult, place the builder's tray on the floor in front of the group.

- Make a show of placing the messy media in the builder's tray and spreading it out.

- Adult takes their 'magic writing finger' (the index finger) and draws out the first letter of one of the children's names.

- Encourage the children to recognise the letter, the child's name and any other words associated with that letter.

- Repeat for the names of all the children in the group.

- When the children are confident and familiar with this activity they can come to the front and write the letters of their friend's names in the messy media.

Finger Fun

RESOURCES

Plasticine or TheraPutty

Marbles

Golf tees

ACTIVITY

- Tell the children that warming up the little muscles in our hand before writing is important and we do the same for our big muscles in PE lessons.

- Model to the children rolling a piece of plasticine into a ball. All do this together.

- Then place your fingers and your thumb together so it looks like a closed beak. Push down onto the top of the plasticine and, as the weight of your fingers starts to go down, slowly open your fingers and stretch them so that the plasticine ends up looking like a ring.

- Then ask all the children to roll the plasticine as a fat sausage. Give each child four golf tees and push these into the plasticine. Then each child gets four marbles and they try to balance these on top of each golf tee.

- The adult places the marbles into the plasticine and rolls them into a ball. The adult gives the plasticine ball to the child. They are only allowed to use a pincer grip (thumb and first finger) to pull the marbles from the plasticine.

Phonic Whispers

RESOURCES

None

ACTIVITY

- Sitting in a circle, sound out either a single letter sound (lower level) or sound out a simple C-V-C word (more able) to the child to your left, whispering to them. (A C-V-C word has the consonant-vowel-consonant.) The child then does the same to the person they are sitting next to and it goes around the group.

- The last person in the group says aloud what they heard.

- Repeat.

Story Basket

RESOURCES

Large basket

Range of small world characters

Range of everyday objects

Selection of pictures of different places

ACTIVITY

- Adult to model taking three items from the basket and saying a sentence out loud. For example, a dragon, a picture of the moon and a toy pizza are chosen: 'The dragon bought pizza on the moon.'

- The children to take turns choosing three items. If they have verbal language they can say a sentence out loud, and if this is still developing, they can put the items in order and the adult can support with the language.

Teaching note: as the children get used to this, offer everyone a whiteboard and encourage them to practise writing the sentences. This can also be themed, based on the topic you are doing.

Can You Find It?

RESOURCES

Children's favourite items hidden around the room

ACTIVITY

- Everyone starts by standing in the middle of the room.

- Adult starts by giving the children one clue, such as 'It is red.'

- The children are then all encouraged to start searching for red things.

- The adult gives a second clue such as 'It has four wheels.'

- The children then start searching for something red with wheels.

- This continues until the children find the correct item and bring it back to the group.

Teaching note: as the children get used to this game, ask them to take a turn at hiding an item and giving their classmates clues.

Story Picture

RESOURCES

Large pieces of paper for each person

Cut out pictures of people, park equipment, etc.

Glue

Pens

ACTIVITY

- Introduce the activity by telling the children that you are going to tell them a story, and that they need to do good listening so they can create a picture of the story.

- Give each child a piece of paper, glue and some pens. Have all the images within reach of all the children.

- Read the following story. Pause after each sentence and support the children to search for characters and actions.

  » One day, Amal was walking. It was a sunny day. Amal saw a park. Amal took a turn on her favourite swing. Then Amal ate an ice cream. It was time to go home.

- Ask the children to share their pictures and retell their story to the group.

Teaching note: keep the story very simple to begin with, and ensure that it is something the children you are working with will have experienced. Give them plenty of time between each sentence. This can be changed to suit any story telling.

SPEAKING

1. Sensory Bingo!

Learning Objective

P4 pupils repeat, copy and imitate between 10 and 50 single words, signs or phrases or use a repertoire of objects of reference or symbols.

Additional Skills

Tactile: tolerating different textures.

Visual: recognising an object matches a picture.

Communication: imitating/repeating/using a word or sign.

Resources

Two bingo boards each with six pictures of different motivating objects, for example Koosh ball, fiddle toy, wind up toy

Objects to match the pictures on the bingo board

Plastic box (preferably clear)

Sensory media – start with textures that are not too challenging for the child, such as cornflakes and shredded paper.

MAIN

- Set up the activity by putting the sensory media in the plastic box and then hiding the objects in among the sensory media. Place the bingo boards next to the box.

- Show the child the box and explain that we need to hunt for objects and match them to our boards; the first one to find all their objects wins!

- Model for the child hunting for an object, finding one, naming it, then matching it to the bingo board.

- Support the child to do the same.

- Every time the child finds an object encourage them to name the object through speech imitation or sign.

- Whoever completes their board first shouts 'Bingo!'

PLENARY

Support the child to put the objects back in the box, labelling each object through speech or sign or indicating the correct picture on the bingo board.

CONSOLIDATION ACTIVITY

Develop the sensory bingo game by using different sensory media and different objects to support the child to develop a wider vocabulary.

2. Ice Ice Rainbow!

Learning Objective

P4 pupils repeat, copy and imitate between 10 and 50 single words, signs or phrases or use a repertoire of objects of reference or symbols.

Additional Skills

Tactile: experiencing different temperatures.

Communication: naming colours using word imitation/symbols/signs.

Attention: attending to an activity for up to five minutes.

Kinaesthetic: working at a different physical level.

Resources

Different coloured paint

Colour symbols to match the colours of the paint

Ice cube tray (ice lolly mould)

Lollipop sticks

Very large piece of white paper

Masking tape

Large picture of a rainbow

MAIN

- Prepare ice painting cubes – the day before the activity pour different coloured paint into ice cube holes in an ice cube tray with a lollipop stick in the middle. Place in the freezer overnight and take out of the freezer just before the activity. Place the very large piece of white paper on the floor and use masking tape to secure the paper to the floor.

- Child and adult sit on the floor together. Look at the large picture of the rainbow and identify the colours together. Encourage the child to imitate the sound or word of the colour. Sing the rainbow song together.

- Show the child a colour symbol, model saying the word and encourage the child to repeat the word.

- Find the colour in the ice cube tray and use the coloured ice cube to make a large arch as the start of your rainbow. Repeat the colour word again.

- Support the child to choose a colour from the symbols, say/imitate the word, find the coloured ice cube and make a large arch to contribute to the rainbow. Encourage the child to say the colour word as they are using it to paint.

- Repeat the activity until a large multicoloured rainbow has been created.

PLENARY

Step back and look at the rainbow together. Support the child to identify the different colours in the rainbow using the symbols or words. Sing the rainbow song together to finish the activity.

CONSOLIDATION ACTIVITY

In different activities such as art or when playing with preferred toys in areas such as the sand tray, encourage the child to identify the colour of an object using words or symbols.

3. Tickle Me More?

Learning Objective

P4 pupils use single words, signs and symbols for familiar objects and to communicate about events and feelings.

Additional Skills

Communication: use words or signs to communicate whether they want to continue or finish a game.

Social communication: enjoying a shared game with a partner.

Tactile: experiencing different sensory input.

Resources

Feather duster (not essential!)

Laminated 'more' and 'finish' symbols

MAIN

- The child and a classmate (or adult role model) sit next to each other opposite the adult.

- First model the game with the classmate or adult role model.

- Sit opposite the child and chant the following rhyme: 'Joe (child's name) is on the chair, Joe is on the chair, Joe is on the chair...UH OH...TICKLE MONSTER!', and use your hands or the feather duster to tickle the child.

- Stop abruptly and wait for the child to indicate whether they want 'more' or to 'finish'. When the child indicates a choice, model using the language and show them the symbol; for example if Joe reaches out his hands, adult says 'Joe wants more!' and shows him the symbol.

- Over time, reduce prompts so that the child is using the symbol or the word to indicate whether they want 'more' of the activity or to 'finish' the activity.

Teaching note: when chanting the song use the inflection in your voice to build up anticipation; for example, start quietly and get louder, and have your hands or feather duster poised in the air ready to tickle!

PLENARY

When the child and classmate are familiar with the game, support the classmate to lead the game.

CONSOLIDATION ACTIVITY

Practise the 'stop', 'go', 'more', 'finish' words with the child in other games; for example, spin the child on an office chair, stop the chair and encourage them to ask for more, or keep spinning the chair and support them to request to stop!

3. Tickle Me More? *cont.*

Teaching note: as practitioners we believe positive contact with children can support relationships and sensory development; however, school policy should be followed when planning this lesson.

4. I'll Tell You What I Want...

Learning Objective

P4 pupils repeat, copy and imitate between 10 and 50 single words, signs or phrases or use a repertoire of objects of reference or symbols.

Additional Skills

Gross motor: engaging in big movements.

Communication: indicating what activity they want next.

Kinaesthetic: moving between different activities.

Resources

Access to PE equipment such as physio ball, A frame, large blanket for swinging, trampette, mats

Symbols for different physical activities laminated and attached by Velcro to a choosing board, for example jumping, rolling, climbing, swinging

MAIN

- Set up the PE equipment in the school hall or in a large, safe area with the different items in different areas of the space.

- Support the child to take off their shoes and socks as independently as possible.

- Model for the child choosing an activity from the symbols, giving the symbol to the other adult and saying the word, for example 'jumping', and then running over to the trampette and jumping.

- Support the child to choose an activity from the symbols, exchange the symbol with an adult and then run over to the equipment needed to engage in the chosen activity.

- When at the activity encourage the child to name the activity they are participating in, for example 'climbing!'

Teaching note: when initially supporting the child to make a choice from symbols that are then given to an adult it is advisable that two adults are available to support this process.

PLENARY

At the end of the session count down '5, 4, 3; 2, 1, PE has finished!' and ask the child to help tidy up the session. Encourage them to name the different pieces of equipment as you tidy them away.

CONSOLIDATION ACTIVITY

Across the day support the child to exchange a symbol for a desired object or activity and model using the word to name the object or activity. Offer specific praise to the child if they use a word, for example 'Great talking!'

5. Farmyard Chat

Learning Objective

P4 pupils use single words, signs and symbols for familiar objects and to communicate about events and feelings.

Additional Skills

Communication: indicating likes and dislikes.

Attention: attending to an activity for up to five minutes.

Fine motor: using a pincer grip to pick up small world toys.

Resources

Small world farm animals

Laminated symbols to match the farm animals being used

A4 piece of paper with a large 'like' symbol

A4 piece of paper with a large 'don't like' symbol

Box or bag

MAIN

- Place all the farm animals in the box or bag.

- Sit across the table from the child and place the like/don't like pieces of paper in front of them.

- Pull an animal out of the bag; identify it by pointing to the symbol and saying the name of the animal.

- Make a show of imitating the animal's noise.

- Make a show of saying you like/don't like the noise the animal makes, and place it on the respective piece of paper.

- Play the game with the child, encouraging them to name the animal that comes out of the bag by either indicating the symbol or using the word.

- Encourage the child to make a noise to represent the animal and then indicate whether or not they like it by placing it on the 'like' or 'don't like' pieces of paper.

PLENARY

Count down '5, 4, 3, 2, 1, farmyard chat has finished' and tidy up the game together. Name the animal and make the noise, as it is placed back in the box or bag.

CONSOLIDATION ACTIVITY

When exploring other activities, such as eating foods at snack time, encourage the child to identify whether they like or don't like the food using 'like' and 'don't like' symbols.

6. Action

Learning Objective

P5 pupils combine single words or symbols to communicate meaning to a range of listeners.

Additional Skills

Social communication: responding to others.

Gross motor: moving the body in a variety of ways.

Attention: increasing attention.

Resources

Two bags

Names of all children laminated with Velcro

Action cards (jump, hop, crawl, etc.) laminated with Velcro

Velcro sentence strip

MAIN

- In the hall, have two bags, one with the children's names and one with the action cards.

- Adult to model taking a name and an action and putting them on the Velcro strip, for example 'Claire jump!' It is then Claire's turn to have a go.

- Repeat so all children have to listen, talk and respond.

PLENARY

At the end of the session, say 'Everyone...' and then pull out an action card.

CONSOLIDATION ACTIVITY

If the children begin getting good at this, put two sets of bags in circulation so that they have to problem solve and listen to more than one set of instructions.

7. Ask for It

Learning Objective

P5 pupils combine single words or symbols to communicate meaning to a range of listeners.

Additional Skills

Social communication: approaching adults to make a request.

Attention: increasing attention.

Resources

Snack items

Symbols to match the snack items

MAIN

- During class snack time ask all the children to sit together at the table.

- Adult to show the children what snack is available, and then to wait.

- When the child makes a request either verbally or with symbols, a small amount will be given to encourage the child to repeat.

- Take the opportunity of a motivating time of the day to encourage as much language and communication as possible.

PLENARY

Ask the children to help to tidy, put away the visuals and help to wash up and clear the table.

CONSOLIDATION ACTIVITY

This strategy can be used in many settings, such as on the playground. The adult can initiate a game such as races or catch, and encourage all children to join in. Adult then stops and waits for the children to request more turns, verbally or using symbols.

8. Red Hat

Learning Objective

P5 pupils combine two key ideas or concepts.

Additional Skills

Visual: tracking and scanning.

Social communication: working in a small group.

Fine motor: manipulating clothing.

Attention: increasing attention.

Resources

Dressing up box

Visuals with colours that are in the box

Visuals of items that are in the box (glasses, hat, ribbon, etc.)

MAIN

- Put on one of the items from the dressing up box and use two key words to describe it, such as 'red hat'.

- Ask an adult in the group to name an item in the box, and the lead adult finds it and puts it on. Move around the group of children.

- Have visuals ready to support the children in sentence structure.

- Once the lead adult has lots of items on, take a photo and ask one of the children to volunteer to dress up.

- All the children take a turn choosing items in which to dress up and using two key words to describe the items.

PLENARY

At the end of the session, ask each child what their favourite item was; allow them to choose this to put on and take a group photo.

CONSOLIDATION ACTIVITY

Print out the photos that you took during the session and have these available with the dressing up clothes and visuals.

9. Run to It

Learning Objective

P5 pupils use a vocabulary of over 50 words.

Additional Skills

Auditory: listening to instructions.

Social communication: acknowledging others and negotiating space.

Gross motor: running.

Resources

Ten PE cones

Ten pictures with familiar items (cat, dog, house, bus, etc.)

MAIN

- Set up cones around the playground; stick a picture on each of the cones.

- Gather all the children in the centre. Adult to model taking a turn by saying aloud one of the pictures.

- The children all run to the picture of the word that has been said.

- Children take turns to be the caller and the others all run to the cones.

PLENARY

As the game is put away, everyone says the name of the item on the picture as they get stacked.

CONSOLIDATION ACTIVITY

Change the pictures regularly; this could be used as a warm up as part of the PE sessions.

10. Take the Red Pen

Learning Objective

P5 pupils combine two key ideas.

Additional Skills

Auditory: listening to instructions.

Social communication: acknowledging others.

Fine motor: using a writing tool.

Kinaesthetic: moving around the paper to reach the desired location.

Resources

Table covered with paper

Pens

Chalk

Crayons

Pictures of each item

MAIN

- Sitting around a table in a small group, place all the art equipment on the table.

- Show one of the children a card illustrating the desired object.

- The child chooses the object and then needs to say '(child's name) (object)' and pass it to them.

- The other child receives the item and makes a response to indicate 'thank you'.

- Repeat this with other members of the group.

- When everyone has two or three art materials, everyone in the group can then start mark-making and drawing.

PLENARY

Sing a tidy up song. Ask the children to help find a place to display their artwork.

CONSOLIDATION ACTIVITY

This activity could be carried out during snack time or a PE lesson, with each of the children naming an object and person.

11. Do as I Say

Learning Objective

P6 pupils can use prepositions such as 'in' or 'on'.

Additional Skills

Auditory: listening to instructions.

Social communication: waiting for a turn.

Fine motor: using a pen.

Kinaesthetic: moving around the paper to reach the desired location.

Resources

Visuals of house, tree, car, swimming pool, café, etc.

Large piece of paper

Marker pens

Small world characters

MAIN

- Lay out a large piece of paper on the floor and have a set of marker pens for everyone to draw.

- Show the children a picture of a house, and ask all the children to draw a house on the paper (this is likely to be mark-making). Place a small visual of a house next to each drawing.

- Then ask the children to repeat this process with a range of objects such as a tree, swimming pool and café. Then tidy up the pens.

- Give each child the chance to choose a figure out of the box.

- Adult to model saying to a child, for example, 'Put the girl next to the house.'

- Work around the group and help to model the sentence structure where needed.

PLENARY

Everyone to say '(Character name) in the box' as they all tidy up the activity.

CONSOLIDATION ACTIVITY

On the playground, take chalk outside and draw a park scene with swings and slides and climbing frames, etc. Ask the children to place themselves 'in the park' and give instructions to each other to move around.

12. Teddy on the Swing

Learning Objective

P6 pupils can use prepositions such as 'in' or 'on'.

Additional Skills

Social communication: responding to others.

Gross motor: moving the body in a variety of ways.

Attention: increasing attention.

Resources

Favourite toys

MAIN

- Ask the children to choose a favourite toy that they can take out to the playground with them. Make sure it is not playtime and that most of the equipment is available.

- When outside allow the children time to explore some of the equipment and the adult to name what they are doing using key words, for example 'Abdul on swing' or 'Jessie under climbing frame'.

- Working around the children one at a time, ask them where their toy wants to play.

- When the child places the toy, ask them to say what they have done, for example 'teddy on slide'.

- Work around the group so each child has a chance to take some turns.

PLENARY

Count down from five to zero and ask all the children to return to class.

CONSOLIDATION ACTIVITY

During the next playtime, ask the children to take turns to provide instructions to their peers about where to go, using prepositions.

13. Come and Play!

Learning Objective

P6 pupils initiate and maintain short conversations using their preferred method of communication.

Additional Skills

Social communication: initiating an interaction with a peer.

Communication: using a recognised form of communication to initiate an interaction.

Attention: maintaining attention to play a game in a small group.

Resources

Laminated symbols of games the child enjoys, for example 'Sensory Bingo' (Lesson 1) or 'In a Twist' (Lesson 26 in *101 Inclusive and SEN Maths Lessons*), velcroed onto choosing board

The resources available for the games a child can choose

Photos or printed names of familiar classmates (depending on level of child)

MAIN

- Support the child to choose a favourite game from the choosing board, name the game and place the symbol for the game in the gap on the sentence strip.

- Working together set up the game so it is ready to play, and encourage the child to comment on the game (for example naming different parts of the game); talk about what they like/don't like about parts of the game.

- When the game is ready, ask the child to pick a friend to come and play by choosing a photo/written name of a familiar friend and place it at the beginning of the sentence strip. The sentence should now read, for example, 'Jen do you want to play bingo with me?'

- Model reading the sentence and support the child to try and say as much of the sentence as possible.

- Support the child to find their chosen friend and support the child to say the sentence to their friend and/or hand them the sentence strip.

- Go and play the game together!

- Support the child to maintain conversation by indicating whose turn it is using the 'my turn' and 'your turn' symbols, and speech where possible.

- Encourage the children to comment on the game as they play.

PLENARY

The child counts down '5, 4, 3, 2, 1, game has finished' and asks their friend to help tidy up using the tidy up sentence strip. Encourage the children to go to the next activity together, for example sand tray, carpet time or maths, and continue interaction.

13. Come and Play! *cont.*

Laminated symbol
sentence '_____
do you want to play
_____ with me?'

Laminated 'my turn' and
'your turn' symbols

'Let's tidy up' symbol
sentence

CONSOLIDATION ACTIVITY

Once the child is familiar with creating a sentence and using it to initiate an interaction with a friend, look for other times in the day where this might be possible, for example using a sentence strip '_____ can I have _____?' to ask for resources such as pencils or paper in small group work. So a sentence might read 'Daniel can I have paper?'

14. Where Oh Where?

Learning Objective

P6 pupils ask simple questions to obtain information.

Additional Skills

Communication: using words or symbols to ask a simple question.

Social communication: working collaboratively in a pair.

Visual: recognising different everyday items and colours.

Resources

Two different coloured bowls and cups

Laminated cup and bowl symbols

Laminated colour symbols to match cup and bowl colours

Two different familiar objects that interest child (e.g. small world duck and cat, train and car)

Laminated sentence strip 'Where is the _____?'

Laminated sentence strip 'Is it under the _____ _____?'

Laminated 'Yes' and 'No' symbols

Finish box

MAIN

- Support the child to choose and invite a friend to come and play with them using the resources from 'Come and Play!' (Lesson 13).

- The children sit opposite each other across a table.

- Child A closes their eyes.

- Child B takes the familiar objects and hides them under different cups/bowls.

- Child A opens their eyes.

- Child B asks, for example, 'Where is the train?' using symbols/speech.

- Child A makes a guess and replies, for example 'Is it under the blue cup?', again using symbols or speech.

- Child B lifts the blue cup and says 'Yes' or 'No' depending on whether the train is there.

- Continue to play until Child A has found both objects.

- Swap over so that both children have the chance to hide the objects.

PLENARY

Tidy up the activity with the children giving each other instructions, for example Child A asks Child B to put the blue cup in the finish box.

CONSOLIDATION ACTIVITY

In other activities such as small world play, maths or English, support the child to ask questions with their peers if they need resources, for example 'Scarlett, where is the calculator?' Support with symbol sentence strips.

15. Mine or Yours?

Learning Objective

P6 pupils can use pronouns correctly.

Additional Skills

Visual: recognising objects that belong to them and those that belong to others.

Communication: using pronouns such as 'mine' and 'yours' correctly.

Social communication: initiating and maintaining an interaction with a classmate.

Resources

Objects/photos of objects that belong to the child and a classmate, for example their school bag, pencil case, coat, pictures of pets/family/house

Box

Laminated 'mine' and 'yours' symbols

Laminated 'my turn' and 'your turn' symbols

MAIN

- Before the activity gather and mix up the objects/photos of the objects that belong to the child and a classmate who they are friends with, and place them in a box.

- Support the child to choose and invite a friend to come and play with them using the resources from 'Come and Play!' (Lesson 13).

- The children sit opposite each other on the carpet or at the table with box next to Child A.

- Before starting the activity, adult models the game. Start by chanting 'Is it mine or yours? Is it mine or yours? Does it belong to you or me? Let's open the box and see!' Adult opens the box and finds an object that belongs to them and explains it is 'mine', indicating the symbol. Chant the song again and this time find an object that belongs to one of the children and explain it is 'yours', again indicating the symbol.

- Chant the song together then Child A reaches into the box to find an object; they then indicate if it is 'mine' or 'yours' using the symbols and/or speech. If it belongs to their friend, hand the object over to them.

- Support Child B to indicate it is their turn by handing the 'my turn' symbol to their friend.

- Chant the song together, then Child B reaches into the box to find an object; they then indicate if it is 'mine' or 'yours' using the symbols and/or speech. If it belongs to their friend, hand the object over to them.

- Continue indicating whose turn it is using the 'my turn' and 'your turn' symbols until all the objects have been sorted.

47

15. Mine or Yours? *cont.*

PLENARY

Quickly place all the objects back into the box and have a 'lightning round'! Adult pulls out the objects from the box quickly and the children indicate if it is theirs using speech or symbols as quickly as they can.

CONSOLIDATION ACTIVITY

At different times of the day, such as before going home, hold up items that belong to the children like coats and bags, and ask 'Whose is this?' Encourage the child to indicate when it is theirs by saying 'mine' or use the name of their classmate to indicate who the item belongs to.

16. Down on the Farm

Learning Objective

P7 pupils use regular plurals correctly.

Additional Skills

Visual: recognising how many animals can be seen.

Communication: using regular plurals and three-key-word sentences to describe how many animals they can see.

Attention: maintaining focus and attention for at least 15 minutes.

Resources

Range of small world farmyard animals: you will need multiples of the same animals and preferably in a range of sizes, for example two small pigs and two big pigs

Laminated animal symbols (using the plural, e.g. chickens, pigs, horses)

Laminated symbols without plurals

Laminated number symbols

MAIN

• Set up the farmyard for the activity with just one set of animals to start with, for example two small pigs and two big pigs.

• With the child look at the animals you can see, and name them.

• Then sing 'Old MacDonald had a farm e-i-e-i-o and on that farm what can you see?'

• Model for the child how to use the sentence strip to make the sentence, for example 'I can see two big pigs.'

• Sing the song again and support the child to use the symbols to make the sentence, for example 'I can see two small pigs.'

• Add more animals to the farm and repeat the sentence building activity.

• As the child gets used to the activity, mix in some of the non-plural animal symbols and support them to hear the difference.

• Then have, for example, one small chicken on the farm and support the child to make the sentence using the non-plural symbol.

• Repeat this with other singular animals and then have multiple animals join the farm and support the child to use the plural symbols correctly.

PLENARY

Line up all the animal symbols (both plural and non-plural) in front of the child. Have a 'lightning round' where you show the child, for example, two chickens and they have to choose between the plural and the non-plural symbol to describe what they are seeing. Next have one horse and repeat. Give specific praise to the child when they are correct, for example 'Fantastic using the plural, Aria!'

16. Down on the Farm *cont.*

Laminated big and small symbols

'I can see _____ _____
_____' laminated
sentence strip

CONSOLIDATION ACTIVITY

When accessing other activities, such as the sand tray, reinforce how to use plurals for the child to hear by holding up 'one spade' and then 'two spades'.

Teaching note: where possible encourage the child to use speech with the symbols when using the plural. Initially make a big show of the 's' sound at the end of a plural so that the child can clearly hear the difference in relation to one object as opposed to multiple objects. When the child starts to use plurals independently, if they make a mistake repeat their sentence back to them using the plural correctly. When they get it right give lots of specific praise.

17. Letter Lotto

Learning Objective

P7 pupils use phrases with up to three key words, signs or symbols to communicate simple ideas, events or stories to others.

Additional Skills

Communication: using up to three key words to describe an object.

Tactile: feeling different textures and shapes.

Social communication: responding appropriately to a partner.

Resources

Feely bag

Range of different coloured/sized letters

Laminated big and small symbols velcroed to a choosing board

Laminated letter symbols velcroed to a choosing board

Laminated colour symbols to match colours of letters going into feely bag, velcroed to choosing board

Laminated sentence strip 'I can see _____ _____ _____'

Two laminated alphabets

MAIN

- Before the activity place all the letters in the feely bag.

- Support the child to choose a friend to come and play.

- Model how to play the game. Sing the following song to the tune of 'Jingle Bells': 'Feely bag, feely bag, what's inside the feely bag? Put your hand in, feel about, when you're ready pull something out!' Pull out a letter from the feely bag and model making and saying the symbol sentence, such as 'I can see big yellow B!', and then matching it to the laminated alphabet.

- Support the children to take it in turns to play. All sing the song together; Child A pulls a letter from the bag, and Child B makes the symbol sentence to describe what they can see and then matches it to their laminated alphabet.

- The first one to complete their alphabet wins!

PLENARY

When the game is finished ask the children to help you tidy up by listening to your instructions. Ask each child in turn to give you the letters from their laminated alphabet using three key words to describe the letters, for example 'George can I have the small blue E?', and place the letters back into the feely bag.

CONSOLIDATION ACTIVITY

When looking at picture books together ask the child to describe what they can see using three key words such as colour, size, quantity and type of character.

18. Tell Me a Tale or Two

Learning Objective

P7 pupils can contribute appropriately one to one and in small group discussions and role play.

Additional Skills

Social communication: collaborating and communicating in a small group.

Communication: contributing appropriately to group discussion and role play.

Auditory: listening and responding to others in a group.

Resources

A copy of the traditional tale 'Hansel and Gretel' – enough copies for at least one between two and a copy for the lead adult

Props for retelling the story: pebbles, bread, bird puppet (or some black material you can wrap around your hand), witch's costume (again using the black material as a cape), cage/box, pretend key

MAIN

- In a small group read the story of Hansel and Gretel together, commenting on the characters and the storyline (also see Lesson 44, 'Traditional Telling').

- When the story is finished explain to the children that they are going to choose a character and act out the story together.

- One at a time the children choose which character they are going to be, using the symbols, and select the correct costume to wear.

- As much as possible allow the group to interact and direct themselves to tell the tale of Hansel and Gretel.

- When the group feel they are ready, film the story. Use the tablet or other video recording device to film the tale being told.

PLENARY

Once the children have taken off their costumes ask them to comment on the experience by responding to questions such as 'Did you like being Hansel?' and 'What is your favourite part of the story?'

CONSOLIDATION ACTIVITY

When learning about or consolidating knowledge about new topics such as the Romans and pirates, support the children to work in a small group to come up with their own characters and a simple story. Work together to tell and film the story.

18. Tell Me a Tale or Two *cont.*

Laminated symbols of each character velcroed to a choosing board

Basic costumes for each character

Tablet or other video recording device

19. The Reviews Are In

Learning Objective

P7 pupils can communicate ideas about past events using simple phrases and statements.

Additional Skills

Communication: using a simple phrase to communicate their ideas about their story.

Social communication: taking part appropriately in a small group discussion.

Auditory: listening and responding to others in a small group.

Resources

The video of the retelling of Hansel and Gretel from Lesson 18, 'Tell Me a Tale or Two'

Interactive whiteboard or equipment to view the video of the story

Laminated 'my turn' and 'your turn' symbols

Laminated sentence prompts such as 'I liked', 'I didn't like', 'I can see'

Laminated photos or written names of classmates taking part in the game

MAIN

- In a small group gather around the whiteboard and get ready to watch the video.

- Make a show about introducing the world premier of Hansel and Gretel starring... (even watch it with popcorn if you can!).

- After viewing the video encourage the children to talk about what they saw, for example who they saw, which character was their favourite, what they did in the story and the parts they liked and didn't like.

PLENARY

Make an advertising poster for the video. The child can attempt to write a sentence about the video or dictate one to an adult to write for them. Put the posters up around the room or in the role play area and let the children have access to the story, props and costumes so that they can role play independently.

CONSOLIDATION ACTIVITY

When other films have been made about other topics, such as the Romans, review the video in the same way, supporting the child to make statements about what they did in the video, who they can see when they are watching it and the parts they did and didn't like.

20. Where Shall They Go?

Learning Objective

P7 pupils can use the conjunction 'and' to link ideas or add new information beyond what is asked.

Additional Skills

Communication: using the conjunction 'and' to link ideas.

Social communication: using prepositions in speech or symbol sentences to give instructions to a classmate.

Kinaesthetic: moving teddy around to different positions.

Resources

Teddy

Doll

Box, chair, cushion

Laminated preposition symbols, for example 'in', 'on', 'under', 'next to', velcroed to a choosing board

Laminated place symbols, for example box, chair, cushion, velcroed to a choosing board

MAIN

- Set up the activity on the carpet or in a quiet space; place the box, cushion and chair in a row with the teddy and doll sat in front of the row of objects.

- Ask the small group of children (maximum four to start with) to sit in a semicircle in front of the objects.

- Choose a child to come to the front (Child A) and ask them to choose a friend (Child B).

- To the tune of 'Farmer's in the Den' sing the song 'Where shall they go? Where shall they go? (Child A's name) tell us where shall they go?'

- Support Child A to make a symbol sentence (using the laminated sentence strip) for Child B to follow, for example 'Child B put teddy on cushion and doll under chair.' Child B then follows the instruction. All celebrate when Child B gets the instruction correct.

- Swap over so that Child B takes on the role of Child A and chooses Child C or D to come and have a turn.

- Play the game until all of the children have had a turn giving and following instructions.

PLENARY

Back in the semicircle, model how to play the 'and' game. Choose a child's name and place it on the '_____ and _____ _____' sentence strip. Choose another child's name and place it after the 'and'; both children stand up. Choose an action, place it on the sentence board and read the whole sentence, for example 'Nancy and James hop!', and the children follow the instruction. Each child then takes it in turns to choose their friends to come and do an action using the sentence strip.

20. Where Shall They Go? *cont.*

Laminated 'teddy' and 'doll' symbols velcroed to a choosing board

Laminated sentence strip '_____ put _____ _____ _____ and _____ ,
_____ _____ _____'

Laminated action symbols (e.g. jump, hop, spin, clap) velcroed to a choosing board

Laminated sentence strip '_____ and _____ _____'

CONSOLIDATION ACTIVITY

Take the 'and' game onto the playground and extend the children and activities that are involved.

Teaching note: during all the sentence building activities make a big show of using the 'and' to emphasise to the child the use of the conjunction.

21. Find a Role Play

Learning Objective

P8 pupils take part in role play with confidence.

Additional Skills

Fine motor: manipulating clothing.

Attention: focusing on an activity for more than 20 minutes.

Resources

Fabric

Themed resources

Images of topic or place

Art supplies (scissors, string, glue, clips, tape)

Pegs

Dressing up clothes

MAIN

- Depending on your classroom theme or topic, set up a role play area. This could be inside or out in the playground/garden.

- Include resources to involve mark-making, dressing up, problem solving, etc. Ask the children to help set this up so that they have ownership.

- Successful set ups can include a space station, a garden centre, a forest and a café.

- Ensure that you leave this out for an extended period.

- Ask the children to bring in items from home or the community to add to the role play.

- Adults always need to model role-play-type behaviours, but not take over the children's play.

PLENARY

At the end of each session, ask the children what role they were and what they would like to do tomorrow.

CONSOLIDATION ACTIVITY

On a local trip, where possible try and visit a setting linked to the role play so that the children can see the roles of others and the purpose that the setting plays in the community.

22. I Need a Coat

Learning Objective

P8 pupils use conjunctions that suggest a cause.

Additional Skills

Fine motor: manipulating clothing.

Attention: focusing for more than 20 minutes.

Auditory: listening to what others have said.

Social communication: providing an appropriate response.

Resources

Large pocket dice with weather pictures in each pocket

Dressing up items for different weathers in a basket

MAIN

- Place the dice in the centre of the group.

- Ask a child to roll the dice. What weather is it showing?

- Ask for a volunteer to be dressed up; they stand in the middle of the group.

- Ask the group 'What do they need to wear?' and when the children respond ask them 'Why?' This should lead on to them starting with 'because', and if they don't the adults can model this.

- Once it is established what type of clothes and why, then someone comes and dresses the volunteer up with the appropriate clothing.

- Another child then takes a turn at rolling the dice and the activity repeats.

PLENARY

Ask the children to take off the dressing up clothes and place these back in the basket.

CONSOLIDATION ACTIVITY

When talking to the children, if they make a comment, begin modelling the 'why/because' question/response phrases so that the children begin to get used to extending their vocabulary.

23. It Was the Puppet

Learning Objective

P8 pupils link up to four key words in communicating or in telling familiar stories.

Additional Skills

Auditory: listening to what others have said.

Social communication: responding appropriately.

Fine motor: cutting and drawing.

Resources

Familiar book

Lolly sticks

Art materials

Action words on sticks, cartoon style

MAIN

- Taking a familiar story, provide all the resources necessary to make lolly stick puppets.

- Each child to make one or two characters from the story.

- Ask the children in the group one by one to describe features of their character.

- Add some key action words, such as 'laughed', 'shouted' and 'stared', that are connected to the story.

- Ask the children to act out the story, using the describing and action words that they have been practising.

PLENARY

Ask all the children to help to tidy away and return all the art materials to their correct location.

CONSOLIDATION ACTIVITY

Place the puppets in the book corner with the book and action words. Leave out some pens and blank action word cards so that the children can write and add more.

24. Puppet Videos

Learning Objective

P8 pupils use an extensive vocabulary to convey meaning to the listener.

Additional Skills

Fine motor: engaging with tablet device.

Attention: focusing for more than 20 minutes.

Auditory: listening to what others have said.

Resources

One tablet device for each child

MAIN

- Download a puppet app to each of the tablet devices you are using.

- Model to the children how the app is used, how they can find images and pictures and how they can record their voice.

- Ask each child to think of an idea for the show they are going to make. Ask them questions such as 'How does it start?' and 'Who are the characters?' to get them thinking through the plot.

- Find quiet spaces for each of the children and allow them 20 minutes to create their show.

- Back as a group, each child gets to present their puppet show video to the class.

- The other children have a chance to ask questions at the end of the video.

PLENARY

Download all the videos and save these. Ask the children to put the tablet devices back.

CONSOLIDATION ACTIVITY

The next time you do this lesson, start by showing these videos and ask the children how they can make them better. Use that as the teaching point for the next video they make.

25. She Needs a Vet

Learning Objective

P8 pupils take part in role play with confidence.

Additional Skills

Auditory: listening to what others have said.

Social interaction: working with others.

Fine motor: manipulating bottle lids.

Resources

Soft toy animals

Medical supplies

Role play items (e.g. telephones, note pads, old computers)

Vet role play items (blankets, name badges, face masks, etc.)

MAIN

- With the children in a group, and the adult holding a toy cat on their lap, tell the children that the cat is sick and needs help.

- Ask the children if they have any ideas what might help.

- Ask the children what helps them when they are sick.

- Together come to the conclusion that the cat needs medical help.

- Ask the children if they know the name of the place (Vets).

- Together, set up the Vets.

- Spend the afternoon adding resources, doing research and putting a vet clinic together.

- Adults to join in so that they are modelling the roles of people that work there.

PLENARY

Let the children know that the animals are sleeping, and that they need to be looked after tomorrow.

CONSOLIDATION ACTIVITY

Keep the role play for at least a week to allow the children to build up role play skills within a familiar setting.

26. Who Does It Belong To?

Learning Objective

P8 pupils can use possessives.

Additional Skills

Auditory: listening to instructions.

Social communication: waiting for a turn and joining in.

Attention: noticing features of others' items.

Resources

Basket

Range of personal belongings from around the class

MAIN

- Collect up a range of the pupils' belongings from around the classroom and place them all in a large basket. Make sure you include adults' belongings also.

- All sitting in a circle, adult to model taking an item out of the bag. Encourage everyone to say 'Who does it belong to?'

- The adult then looks around the group and back at the item and says, for example, 'Adam's bag' and gives the bag to Adam.

- Pass the basket to the next person. Encourage all members of the group to ask the question and the child to verbally (or by any other means) answer the question.

PLENARY

Everyone to put their belongings back in the correct place.

CONSOLIDATION ACTIVITY

This can be done at the end of the day; an adult can go with the child to help pack the bags, using the same key question and waiting for the child to respond.

LISTENING

27. Noisy Beanbag

Learning Objective

P4 pupils demonstrate an understanding of at least 50 words, including the names of familiar objects.

Additional Skills

Gross motor: throwing and catching.

Social communication: following rules.

Communication: responding with vocalisations or words to another person.

Attention: increasing attention.

Resources

Beanbag

MAIN

- Everyone in the group sits on a chair in a circle.
- The leader of the group has a beanbag and throws it to a member of the group, saying their name.
- Everyone takes a turn.
- When the leader gets it back, they say an animal name, such as a cow, and everyone that catches the beanbag makes the noise of the animal.
- Continue playing this for around 5–10 minutes.

PLENARY

Say goodbye to each person in the group by passing the beanbag around one last time.

CONSOLIDATION ACTIVITY

This can be played on the playground with a football or tennis ball during the starter of a PE session.

28. Paint by Colour

Learning Objective

P4 pupils demonstrate an understanding of at least 50 words, including the names of familiar objects.

Additional Skills

Visual: recognising colours and words.

Attention: maintaining concentration until a task is complete.

Fine motor: painting with brush.

Resources

Large pieces of paper

Aprons

Red, yellow, green and blue paint and brushes

Access to music

Visuals of red, yellow, green and blue paint, ideally A4

MAIN

- Set up the room ready for the art session. Put the aprons on each chair, and have the paint and the brushes on the table and the large piece of paper.

- Put on a piece of relaxing music in the background; the children will use this as inspiration.

- When the session starts, support each of the children to put on their apron and find a seat.

- Adult to show the children a colour visual (such as red) and ask each of the children to identify the red paint. Everyone, including the adult, paints with red paint to the music.

- Change the colours and the music so that you create different experiences.

PLENARY

Tidy up together, put the aprons in the wash basket, wash up the paint and the brushes and hang out the painting to dry.

CONSOLIDATION ACTIVITY

On the playground, place a large piece of paper and lots of chalk. Use the same visuals to support the children generalising their understanding of colours.

29. Match It

Learning Objective

P4 pupils respond appropriately to simple requests which contain one key word, sign or symbol in familiar situations.

Additional Skills

Visual: tracking and scanning.

Social communication: working in a small group.

Kinaesthetic: moving around the room.

Attention: increasing attention.

Resources

Picture and word labels of key classroom items (e.g. paint, coats, sink, cups, paper)

MAIN

• To start this lesson, have a few items on the table with the labels, and model to the children saying the word on the label and matching it to the correct item.

• Working in pairs or small groups, everyone is given a label of a classroom item; the word is said and the children need to go and find the item, stick the label on and come back to the leader for another label.

PLENARY

As a larger group, walk around the class and look at all the new labels. If one is in the wrong place, model to the child 'Uh oh, is this _____?' and replace it where it needs to be in the room.

CONSOLIDATION ACTIVITY

If working in mixed-ability groups assign the children different roles; for example the leader can say the word, the child that can write could write the label and then together the group can go and find the item in the room. Each person in the group needs to be assigned a role so that one person does not take over: writer, finder, placer.

30. Roll It, Do It

Learning Objective

P4 pupils respond appropriately to simple requests which contain one key word, sign or symbol in familiar situations.

Additional Skills

Visual: recognising symbol and word.

Gross motor: using the body in a variety of ways.

Social communication: working as part of a small group.

Resources

Large pocket dice

Symbols and words on paper that fit in the dice (e.g. jumping, hopping, clap, bunny hops)

MAIN

- Everyone sits in a circle, leaving space in the middle to carry out the actions.

- One by one, each person rolls the dice.

- They look at the top symbol and word and they are supported by the adult to say the word.

- The person then carries out the action and passes the dice to the next person.

PLENARY

The leader of the group rolls the dice one last time, and everyone carries out the action together. Then say '5, 4, 3, 2, 1, *Roll It, Do It* has finished.'

CONSOLIDATION ACTIVITY

To extend this activity, add a second dice with numbers (1–3) so that the child is having to recognise an action and complete it a set amount of times.

31. Traffic Lights

Learning Objective

P4 pupils demonstrate an understanding of at least 50 words, including the names of familiar objects.

Additional Skills

Visual: negotiating space with others.

Gross motor: running, walking and stopping.

Social communication: working as part of a small group.

Resources

Red card with the word 'stop'

Orange card with the word 'walk'

Green card with the word 'run'

MAIN

- This game just needs a big space that the children can run around in, and ideally the coloured cards to support the language that is used.

- As a group, model the actions. Red is stop, orange is walk and green is run.

- Ensure that you have some more adults in the group so that they can model this alongside the children.

- Initially, only say 'stop', 'walk', and 'run'. Don't confuse the children by adding the colours. Once they get used to the language and the game, these can be added.

- Play this game for around ten minutes.

PLENARY

Do some cool down stretches and talk about the names of the different (simple) body parts.

CONSOLIDATION ACTIVITY

Once the children have got used to the commands, let them take turns at leading the game. You need the coloured cards so that if they are not yet talking they can still indicate the action they want everyone to take.

32. Next to the Fridge

Learning Objective

P5 pupils follow requests and instructions containing at least two key words, signs or symbols.

Additional Skills

Fine motor: manipulating the different props.

Social communication: working as part of a small group.

Attention: increasing attention to 10–15 minutes.

Communication: using verbal expression or symbols to make a request of another person.

Resources

Dolls' house

Range of dolls (three)

Range of furniture (four)

Symbols (all with soft Velcro on the back): every doll, all furniture items, each room and 'in', 'on', 'next to', 'under'

Sentence strip (an A5 laminated piece of card with a strip of hard Velcro horizontally)

MAIN

- Have a dolls' house on the table, with the box of furniture and dolls next to it.

- Invite children to come and play. This will work well with either one to one or a small group of two, depending on how big the dolls' house is.

- Adult to model a sentence 'Put daddy doll in the kitchen' and carry out the action.

- Adult to then provide a request to the child by adding the visuals to a sentence strip so that they can refer back, for example 'Mummy in bedroom'.

- Spend time making requests of the child(ren) and then allow them to make requests of the adult.

PLENARY

At tidy up time, adult to make a request, (e.g. 'Baby in the box') and child to make a request (e.g. 'Toilet in the box') either verbally or with symbols – until everything is put away.

CONSOLIDATION ACTIVITY

This activity can be carried out with a number of different role play set ups, such as a castle, train station and doctor's surgery. This will support the child to generalise the skill of following two-word instructions.

33. Three Bowls of Porridge

Learning Objective

P5 pupils follow requests and instructions containing at least two key words, signs or symbols.

Additional Skills

Fine motor: manipulating the different props.

Social communication: working as part of a small group.

Auditory: listening to the story.

Attention: increasing attention to 10–15 minutes.

Resources

'Goldilocks and the Three Bears' book

Three different size bears

Three bowls and spoons

Three chairs

Three beds

MAIN

- Read the story of 'Goldilocks and the Three Bears' to the group – no more than three children.

- Present to the group the three bears, and ask the children one by one to take either the daddy bear, mummy bear or baby bear.

- Have all the resources ready from the list.

- Verbally work through different scenarios in the story, for example 'Baby bear wants a bowl', and give the child time to carry out the request.

PLENARY

Have one last read-through of the story, where the children have the props, and give them a chance to play along with the story.

CONSOLIDATION ACTIVITY

Place the book and the props in a story box that the children can have access to across a week so that they can explore.

34. Tiger Needs a Dress

Learning Objective

P5 pupils follow requests and instructions containing at least two key words, signs or symbols.

Additional Skills

Visual: searching for desired item.

Social communication: waiting for a turn.

Fine motor: manipulating fastenings and props.

Resources

Range of characters (e.g. teddy, doll, tiger)

Range of props (dress, bowl, hat, cup, etc.)

Picture cards of each of the above items

MAIN

- For this session, the adult needs to sit one side of the table and the children on the other side, so that the children do not need to wait too long for a turn.

- Place the two piles of cards face down on the table. Adult asks a child to turn one card from each pile and says a sentence. For example, if doll and dress were turned over, the adult would say 'The doll wants the dress.' Give the child time to respond and, if they need it modelling, show them searching through the box and carrying out the request.

- Once the first child has turned two cards over and is searching for the items, move on to the next child in the group so that they can turn two cards over and the adult can model the sentence. Ensure that the cards are left with the children so that they can refer back.

PLENARY

Once everyone has been doing the activity for around ten minutes, work back through the group, read the sentence and look at the items that the child has chosen. If they are correct everyone can cheer, and if they are incorrect say 'Uh oh, let's look again', supporting the child and then cheering.

CONSOLIDATION ACTIVITY

Once the children have done this lesson a few times, they can work more independently at this, and it could be sent home as a practice activity.

35. What's That Noise?

Learning Objective

P5 pupils respond appropriately to questions about familiar events.

Additional Skills

Kinaesthetic: shaking the containers.

Social communication: following rules.

Attention: increasing attention.

Resources

Opaque containers (with lids) filled with different noisy items such as rice, marbles, little bells, pasta, sequins, paper clips

Choosing board with a picture of each of the fillings

MAIN

• Working individually to begin with, the containers are laid out across the table.

• Give the child a chance to shake them, listen and explore.

• Present the child with the choosing board. Adult asks 'What's that noise?'

• Adult to model shaking the container and matching it to the correct picture.

• Once the child has played this a few times, introduce more children, so they can take turns at listening and matching.

PLENARY

Shake each container as it is put away, and ask children in the group to either say or point to what the sound is.

CONSOLIDATION ACTIVITY

The next time you do this, the adult can show a small group of children the picture of what they want them to find, and ask 'Can you find the same?' The children have to shake the containers to find the correct one.

36. Where's Teddy?

Learning Objective

P5 pupils respond appropriately to questions about familiar or immediate events.

Additional Skills

Visual: scanning the area.

Social communication: waiting for a turn.

Attention: increasing attention to 10–15 minutes.

Resources

Teddy bear

Beanbag

Music

MAIN

• Sitting in a circle, tell the group that we are going to play hide and seek.

• Ask everyone in the group to close their eyes and the leader to go and hide the teddy. The children are likely to need support with this.

• When leader is back in the group, the music starts and the beanbag is passed around. When the music stops, that person gets a turn at finding teddy.

• Ask the child 'Where is teddy?' and support the child finding it as much as necessary.

• For each child make this simpler/harder as necessary.

PLENARY

To finish the game, take the beanbag and pass it around the group; each person has to say their name. On the next time around, they then throw the beanbag to another person in the group, saying their name, meaning everyone needs to be listening!

CONSOLIDATION ACTIVITY

In everyday classroom situations, ask the child to go and find items that they need in order to carry out their work or tasks.

37. Parachute Ball

Learning Objective

P6 pupils respond to others in group situations.

Additional Skills

Kinaesthetic: running under the parachute.

Gross motor: passing ball to another child.

Social communication: waiting for classmate, responding to classmate.

Auditory: listening and responding to own name and understanding names of others.

Resources

Parachute

Ball

MAIN

- Stand around the parachute in a small group.

- Adults lift up parachute and waft.

- One child has the ball.

- Adult calls out another child's name; child runs to the named child and passes the ball and says another child's name.

- Keep going around the group saying different names and passing the ball to each other.

PLENARY

Put the parachute on the floor; everyone sits around the edge of the parachute. Throw the ball from one to another over the parachute shouting the name of the child you are throwing to.

CONSOLIDATION ACTIVITY

Across the day encourage each child to interact and respond to others; for example at the end of the day ask child to hand out bags/coats to their friends, following instructions such as 'Give the coat to Fred.'

38. Shopkeeper

Learning Objective

P6 pupils respond to others in group situations.

Additional Skills

Communication: listening and responding to classmates.

Auditory: processing requests from others.

Social communication: initiating and responding to interaction with classmates or adults.

Resources

Snack items

Words/symbols/pictures that match snack items velcroed on choosing board

Table/role play shop

MAIN

- Set up the snack shop using a table or role play shop with snack items next to the 'shopkeeper' and the choosing board at front of shop/table.

- Ask the child to sit in the shopkeeper seat.

- Encourage classmates to come to the shop, select an item from the snack choosing board and give the word/picture/symbol to the shopkeeper using a phrase such as '(Child's name) can I have a banana?'

- Shopkeeper takes the word/symbol/picture from their classmate, finds the selected snack and gives it to their classmate, using a phrase such as '(Classmate's name) here is your banana.'

- Encourage classmates to come and choose a snack and continue the interaction.

PLENARY

Swap roles at the 'shop' so that the child is the one asking for snack items from their classmates.

CONSOLIDATION ACTIVITY

Set up a 'shop' in the outside area selling items for messy play, for example buckets and spades for the sand tray, trains and tracks for the train set, and support the child to play shopkeeper, listening and responding to their classmates' requests.

39. Human Shape Sorter

Learning Objective

P6 pupils follow requests and instructions with three key words, signs or symbols.

Additional Skills

Gross motor: moving body into different positions.

Auditory: listening to and following three key word instructions.

Social communication: working in a small group.

Tactile: tolerating others nearby.

Resources

Large laminated square, circle and triangle (three) in three different colours, for example red (square, circle, triangle), blue (square, circle, triangle), yellow (square, circle, triangle)

Blu Tack

Laminated symbols matching colours and shapes (for example red, blue, yellow, square, circle, triangle) with soft Velcro on the back

MAIN

- Blu Tack the laminated shapes securely to the floor in colour lines (all the blue shapes in a line, all the red shapes in a line, all the yellow shapes in a line) to make a square on the floor.

- Child chooses a partner to work with.

- Child A stands one side of the shape square, Child B stands on the other side.

- Adult or another classmate chooses a colour symbol, shape symbol and a hand or foot symbol to make an instruction such as 'hand red square'.

- Child A places hand on red square.

- Adult or classmate selects three more symbols, for example 'foot blue triangle'.

- Child B follows the instructions.

- Continue playing the game following the three key word instructions until one child tumbles over!

- Swap roles and play again.

PLENARY

Child helps to tidy up following instructions, for example 'Red triangle in tray', 'Blue circle in bag'.

CONSOLIDATION ACTIVITY

In the playground draw out the shape square using different coloured playground chalk and encourage the child to play the game with different friends.

39. Human Shape Sorter *cont.*

Laminated symbols of hand and foot with soft Velcro on the back

A laminated strip long enough to line up three symbols with hard Velcro

Tray

Bag

Playground chalk

40. Dress It Up!

Learning Objective

P6 pupils follow requests and instructions with three key words, signs or symbols.

Additional Skills

Fine motor: dressing skills.

Auditory: listening to and following three key word instructions.

Social communication: working in a small group.

Resources

A doll and a teddy of similar size

Range of dressing up clothes in different colours and sizes, for example big and small t-shirt, pink and blue gloves

Colour symbols that match colours of dress up clothes with soft Velcro on the back

Laminated symbols that match type of dress up clothes with soft Velcro on the back

Laminated big and small symbols with soft Velcro on the back

MAIN

- Adult sets up the activity either on the table or carpet with the doll and teddy sat next to each other and the dressing up clothes clearly laid out.

- Child A chooses a partner to work with.

- Adult models making a three-key-word instruction by lining up the symbols on the laminated strip, for example 'Big jumper teddy'.

- Child A follows instructions to dress teddy up in the big jumper.

- Child A then selects three symbols for Child B to follow, for example 'Red shoes doll'.

- Continue taking turns dressing up the doll and teddy.

- Encourage children to comment on how the doll or teddy looks in the clothes.

PLENARY

Child helps to tidy up following instructions, for example 'Put red jumper in bag' and 'Put doll in box'.

CONSOLIDATION ACTIVITY

Play the same game but with a bigger group and this time use the children instead of a doll and teddy.

40. Dress It Up! *cont.*

Laminated doll and teddy symbols with soft Velcro on the back

Laminated strip long enough to line up three symbols with hard Velcro

Bag/box/tray

41. Where Have You Gone?

Learning Objective

P6 pupils respond to others in group situations.

Additional Skills

Attention: watching their classmates take a turn.

Social communication: waiting a turn, understanding when to take a turn.

Auditory: listening to instructions to take a turn, joining in with familiar rhyme.

Tactile: experiencing the feeling of the texture of the blanket and being in the dark.

Resources

Piece of material/blanket large enough to cover a child

Chair

Photos of children in the group, if needed, for the child to indicate whose turn is next

MAIN

- Children sit in a small group in a semicircle.
- Place the chair at the front of the group.
- Ask two children to come to the front.
- Ask Child A to come and sit on the chair.
- Place the blanket over the child and sing to the tune of 'Frère Jacques': 'Where is Child A? Where is Child A? I don't know! I don't know! Child B, can you find them? Child B, can you find them?' Child B pulls off the blanket then sings 'There he/she is! There he/she is!'
- Child B swaps with Child A to sit on the chair; Child A chooses a friend to come and take a turn with the blanket.
- As the children become familiar with the game the adult can step back and allow the group to manage the game independently.

Teaching note: as you are playing the game ask the group questions such as 'Who has not had a turn?' to encourage their group attention skills.

PLENARY

Ask the children to close their eyes. Quietly select one child from the group to come and sit on the chair and cover them up with the blanket. Ask the children to open their eyes and identify which of their classmates is under the blanket!

CONSOLIDATION ACTIVITY

In small group activities across the day encourage the child to name the members that are in their group and identify if a child is not there or comment on where they have gone.

42. Search Far and Wide

Learning Objective

P7 pupils follow requests and instructions with four key words, signs or symbols.

Additional Skills

Kinaesthetic: moving about the school/local community.

Auditory: processing and responding to four key word instructions.

Attention: maintaining focus to complete activity.

Communication: responding appropriately to four key word instructions.

Resources

Laminated symbols of places in school/community, for example library, reception, shop, park, with soft Velcro on the back

Laminated symbols of different objects found in the places, for example book, pen, paper, apples, flowers, with soft Velcro on the back

MAIN

- Explain to the child that you need help as lots of items have gone missing and you need help to find them!

- Line up four of the symbols, for example 'four red apples shop'.

- Support the child to go on a hunt for the items.

- Once an item is found line up four more symbols and hunt again, for example 'two yellow flowers park'.

Teaching note: going out in the local community is a great opportunity to practise listening skills such as stopping and waiting at traffic lights, responding to directions, etc. However, if it's not possible to go out in the community, hunt around the school instead.

PLENARY

Once returned to the classroom ask the child to recount the items they found and where they found them, using words or symbols.

CONSOLIDATION ACTIVITY

Across the day build in opportunities for the child to process four key word instructions, for example 'Sit on carpet on big, red triangle.'

42. Search Far and Wide *cont.*

Laminated adjective symbols, for example big/small, colours, long/short, etc. with soft Velcro on the back

Laminated number symbols with soft Velcro on the back

Laminated symbols that might describe a particular object, for example a dinosaur for a Dinosaur book

Laminated strip long enough to line up four symbols with a line of hard Velcro

43. Cups of Wonder

Learning Objective

P7 pupils attend to and respond to questions from adults and their peers about experiences, events and stories.

Additional Skills

Visual: tracking an object as it is placed and moved.

Social communication: responding appropriately to an interaction with a classmate.

Communication: indicating where the object had gone.

Resources

A motivating object such as a Koosh ball or wind up toy

Three different coloured cups or bowls (depending on size of motivating object)

Laminated arrow (or 'middle', 'right' and 'left' symbols depending on understanding of child)

MAIN

- Support child to choose a classmate to join them in the lesson.

- Children sit one side of the table, adult on the other side.

- Adult lines up the three cups/bowls and make a big show of hiding the object under the cups/bowls then move them around.

- Ask the children 'Where has the object gone?' Encourage them to use the arrow to indicate where the object has gone.

- Swap around so that each child has the chance to hide and move the object as well as find it.

PLENARY

Add another object to the activity so that the questions can be extended, for example 'Where is the red ball?'

CONSOLIDATION ACTIVITY

In the playground play games such as hide and seek, but with eyes open, and encourage child to respond to questions such as 'Where has Bill gone?' before going to find them.

44. Traditional Telling

Learning Objective

P7 pupils listen, attend to and follow stories for short stretches of time.

Additional Skills

Auditory: listening and responding to a familiar story.

Communication: indicating what is next in the story.

Attention: increasing joint attention skills to 10–15 minutes.

Resources

A copy of the traditional tale 'Hansel and Gretel' – enough copies for at least one between two and copy for the lead adult

Props for retelling the story: pebbles, breadcrumbs, bird puppet (or some black material you can wrap around your hand), witch's costume (again using the black material as a cape), cage/box, boy and girl dolls, pretend key

MAIN

- Children sit in a small group in a semicircle, so every child can see a copy of the story. This activity will need other adults who can support the children to turn the pages of the book and follow the story.

- The lead adult stands in front of the group and models opening the book and reading the first page. Pace your language so it is clear, and be dramatic in your delivery to maintain children's attention.

- Adult acts out the story using the props:

  » Lay the pebbles and then return back home.

  » Drop the breadcrumbs then use the bird puppet/ black material to eat them up.

  » Witch's costume/black material to enact the part of the witch.

  » Place the boy doll in the cage/box.

  » Girl doll uses key to release boy doll from cage/ box.

- Lead adult uses the whole of the front of the semicircle to enact the story while the children follow using their own copies.

PLENARY

Once the story has finished ask each child to come to the front and enact their favourite part using the appropriate prop.

CONSOLIDATION ACTIVITY

Using lollipop sticks and cut out pictures of the characters, children can make their own story characters and re-enact the story in small groups. This could be filmed and watched back as a group.

45. Out and About

Learning Objective

P7 pupils attend to and respond to questions from adults and their peers about experiences, events and stories.

Additional Skills

Auditory: listening and responding appropriately to questions about an experience.

Visual: recognising self and familiar others in photos.

Communication: commenting appropriately on the photos.

Resources

Photos from a recent trip or exciting experience, for example going to the zoo or science day

Symbols that match what is happening in the photos; for example if the photos are of a zoo trip have symbols of the animals seen, the names of the children in the photos and actions that might be captured in the photos such as walking, running and climbing

'Like'/'don't like' symbols

MAIN

- Support Child A to choose a friend to come and look at the trip photos with them.

- At the table look at the photos together. Adult models asking clear, simple questions about the photos that can be answered using the provided symbols, for example 'What animal can you see?' and 'Who is eating their lunch?'

- Adult encourages Child B to ask questions of Child A about the trip photos and supports Child A to respond to the questions appropriately using speech or symbols.

PLENARY

After looking at the photos and responding to questions about them, support Child B to ask Child A if they liked or didn't like the trip and encourage Child A to respond using speech or symbols.

CONSOLIDATION ACTIVITY

Repeat this activity using photos of everyday routines and other interesting events, each time encouraging the child to respond to questions from their peers using speech or symbols.

46. On and Under

Learning Objective

P7 pupils follow requests and instructions with four key words, signs or symbols.

Additional Skills

Kinaesthetic: moving body into different positions.

Auditory: processing and responding to four key word instructions.

Social communication: waiting for a turn in a small group.

Resources

Laminated pictures/ names of children chosen to work in a small group

Laminated position word symbols with soft Velcro on the back, for example 'in', 'under', 'on', 'next to', 'behind'

Laminated 'big'/'small' symbols with soft Velcro on the back

Range of PE equipment such as A frames, benches, different size balls

Matching laminated PE equipment symbols with soft Velcro on the back

MAIN

• In the hall set up the PE equipment so that there are different sized (and if possible coloured) A frames, benches and balls set up around the room.

• When the small group of children comes to the hall have them sit down in a line facing the equipment.

• Adult models placing four symbols on the laminated strip to create a four-key-word instruction, for example 'Heidi on small A frame.'

• Child listens for their name then follows the instructions.

• Children take it in turns to make instruction sentences for each other and run around the room following the different instructions.

PLENARY

Children help to tidy up the PE equipment following instructions, for example 'Ben put yellow ball in cupboard.'

CONSOLIDATION ACTIVITY

Out in the playground encourage children to play a similar game but using the playground equipment and actions instead, for example 'Laura jump on roundabout!' and 'Jack stand under slide!'

46. On and Under *cont.*

Laminated colour symbols to match PE equipment with soft Velcro on the back

Laminated strip long enough to line up four symbols with hard Velcro

47. Roll Play

Learning Objective

P8 pupils take part in role play with confidence.

Additional Skills

Gross motor: rolling the dice.

Communication: extended interactions.

Social communication: responding appropriately to others in a group.

Resources

Two large pocket dice: one with different role play scenes, for example hospital, space ship, home corner, one with blank sides

Laminated cards with different characters from role play scenes, for example doctor, patient, nurse, astronaut, alien

Matching dressing up and props for chosen role play scenes

MAIN

- In a small group choose one child to roll the pocket dice containing the role play scenes.

- When the dice lands, quickly place the relevant character cards in the pockets of the other dice.

- Each child takes a turn to roll the character dice revealing who they will play in role play (take each card out as it is rolled to avoid doubling up!).

- Encourage the children to dress up and find the relevant props for their character and then take part in the role play.

- Adult supports the play by either rolling a character themselves or introducing new ideas, for example 'The doctor bumped his head! Oh no, who can help?'

PLENARY

Use a timer to show the group how long they have left of the current role play scene. When the timer is done count down, for example '5, 4, 3, 2, 1, hospital has finished!' And encourage the group to tidy up the resources and dressing up into the correct bags/boxes. Then choose another child to roll the role play dice and repeat the activity again.

CONSOLIDATION ACTIVITY

Take photos of the children taking part in the role play games and make class books with the photos. Share the books with the child and encourage them to comment on the role play, what was happening, who their friends played, etc.

48. What Happened to Baby?

Learning Objective

P8 pupils listen attentively. They respond appropriately to questions about why or how.

Additional Skills

Auditory: responding appropriately to questions from an adult or classmate.

Tactile: experiencing different sensory media.

Communication: using speech or symbols to respond appropriately to questions.

Resources

Plastic baby

Baby role play items, for example clothes, bath, bottle

Laminated symbols with soft Velcro on the back that indicate why baby might be feeling a certain way, for example 'bath', 'hungry', 'thirsty', 'mud', 'no clothes', 'wet'

MAIN

- Introduce the child to the baby and model playing with the baby, for example 'Baby is crawling. Oh no! She crawled in the mud – now she is dirty!'
- Ask the child 'Why is baby dirty?' and support them to answer using speech or symbols, for example 'She went in the mud' or indicating the mud symbol.
- Play with the baby together and ask questions as you go along, for example[AQ] 'Why is baby wet?' ('She went in the bath') 'Why is baby crying? ('She's hungry') and 'Why is baby cold?' ('No clothes').

Teaching note: as the child gets used to this game and to responding to questions, introduce the idea of asking how baby is feeling once she is clean, dry and fed.

PLENARY

Pretend the baby is yawning and ask the child why the baby is yawning. Support the child to answer that the baby is sleepy. Put the baby to bed and count down from five to one to finish the activity.

CONSOLIDATION ACTIVITY

When the child is expressing how they are feeling ask them why they are feeling like that; for example if child is saying they want to change an item of clothing, such as their top, ask them why (it might be because it is dirty, wet, etc.).

49. Act It Out

Learning Objective

P8 pupils take part in role play with confidence.

Additional Skills

Kinaesthetic: moving body around into different positions.

Cognitive: thinking about how to represent a word/symbol/picture with body movements.

Social communication: standing in front of a small group.

Communication: developing non-verbal communication skills.

Resources

Laminated words/symbols/pictures of very familiar and motivating objects to child that are simple to represent with body movements, for example pets/animals, actions, vehicles

Bowl

MAIN

- Children sit in a small group in a semicircle.
- Adult models reaching into the bowl, choosing a word/symbol/picture and then acting out the word/symbol/picture while the children guess what it is; for example if the word/symbol/picture is a rabbit, adult acts like a rabbit while children guess what they are doing.
- Children then take it in turns to choose a word/symbol/picture from the bowl and act it out for the group.
- Either the first child to guess has the next turn or the child who did the acting can choose a friend.

PLENARY

Adult sits at the front of the group with the bowl of words/symbols/pictures. Adult picks up a word/symbol/picture and shows it to the group without looking. All the children in the group act out the word/symbol/picture and the adult has to guess! Swap around so children have a turn sitting on the chair and choosing.

CONSOLIDATION ACTIVITY

When the child is happy and calm but is asking for something familiar such as a drink or a spade for the sand tray, encourage them to act out what it is that they want (in order to develop their non-verbal communication skills).

50. If the Hat Fits

Learning Objective

P8 pupils take part in role play with confidence.

Additional Skills

Visual: selecting the correct prop.

Social communication: waiting for a turn and negotiating.

Attention: increasing attention to 20 minutes.

Resources

Hats (police, fire, nurse, crown, cowboy, pirate, astronaut)

Scenario cards (space, police chase, building on fire, procession, horses, treasure on an island, hospital)

MAIN

- Have the dressing up box in the middle of the room.
- Tell the group that today we need to pretend to be someone else.
- Leader of the group to model showing the scenario card of treasure on an island, looking through the basket and finding a pirate hat. Leader then acts out the pirate voice and being mean.
- If you have enough of each hat for everyone to take a turn together, then on the next card you ask everyone to go and find the hat. If you only have one of each, ask each of the children to choose a hat, and come and find their scenario card.
- When each member of the group is in character, model being that character and putting on the voices.
- Can the children find any other props in the room that might help them (e.g. a parrot for the pirate, a clipboard for the nurse, handcuffs for the police officer)?

PLENARY

Ask the children to tidy up all the hats, and put any props away. Then ask one of the children to go to the book corner and find a book about a character they have played. Read this as a group.

CONSOLIDATION ACTIVITY

Place the basket of hats in the book corner, and find as many books that go with the characters as possible. Have these as the key texts so that the children build understanding about the types of activities the different characters do.

51. Pig Spoons

Learning Objective

P8 pupils take part in role play with confidence.

Additional Skills

Fine motor: manipulating materials to make puppet.

Social communication: working with others.

Communication: speaking clearly, or using assistive technology to compose a sentence.

Attention: increasing attention to 20 minutes.

Resources

Wooden spoons

'Three Little Pigs' story

Art materials to create puppets (paint, glitter, glue, scissors, felt, etc.)

MAIN

- Read the story 'Three Little Pigs' together as a group.

- Then tell the children that we need to make some puppets so that we can act out the story.

- Each child has a wooden spoon and they decide if they want to be a pig or the wolf.

- Spend time looking at the range of pictures of a pig and wolf; what are the key characteristics?

- Allow the children 15 minutes at the art table to make their puppet.

- When all the puppets are made, come back to the group. If some of them are very wet, then use a stand-in for the first time until it dries.

- Act out the story all together.

PLENARY

Tidy up time.

CONSOLIDATION ACTIVITY

Children to practise this, and then it could be acted out either for another class, or for the assembly.

52. Tape It

Learning Objective

P8 pupils respond appropriately to question about what or how.

Additional Skills

Fine motor: controlling a tablet device.

Social communication: understanding roles.

Communication: speaking clearly.

Attention: increasing attention to 20 minutes.

Resources

Lego

Tablet device

Question prompts

MAIN

- In groups of two, the children demonstrate building a Lego model.

- The first child in the pair builds the model; the second child films this on a tablet device.

- Together they watch the video, and the second child is given a question prompt sheet to ask the first child questions. Questions may include 'How many bricks did you use?' or 'Why did you choose those colours?' Adults may need to model this process.

- Swap over and the roles change.

PLENARY

A few children can share their videos with the group, and the group can ask questions.

CONSOLIDATION ACTIVITY

During the next whole class lesson, an adult could film the session. After this, the video can be shown to the whole class and children take turns at asking and answering questions.

READING

53. More Please!

Learning Objective

P4 pupils listen and respond to familiar rhymes and stories.

Additional Skills

Kinaesthetic: rocking back and forth, stopping and starting.

Social communication: indicating wanting more through eye contact/ gesture/verbalisation.

Auditory: listening to the rhyme and noticing changes, for example when the rhyme stops.

Communication: choosing between two objects.

Resources

Small plastic boat

Toy spider

MAIN

- Present the child with the boat and the spider and encourage them to choose (this might be through reaching out, verbalisation or eye gaze).

- When the child makes a choice, label their choice, for example 'Boat! Row, row, row your boat.'

- Sing the chosen rhyme, pausing at crucial moments to allow the child to respond to request more of the action through eye contact, gesture (such as pulling your hand) or verbalisation.

  » Row Your Boat: Hold the child's hands, rock back and forth and sing 'Row, row, row your boat gently down the stream/river/to the shore/brook, if you see a crocodile/polar bear/lion/gorilla, don't forget to (PAUSE and WAIT) scream/shiver (shake arms)/roar/look.'

  » Incy Wincy Spider: With child sat on chair or carpet, sing 'Incy Wincy spider climbed (PAUSE and WAIT) up the water spout (tickle fingers up outside of child's legs), down came the (PAUSE and WAIT) rain and washed the spider out (sweeping motion down outside of child's arms), out came the (PAUSE and WAIT) sunshine and dried up all the rain (using flat palm, make circular motions on child) and Incy Wincy Spider climbed (PAUSE and WAIT) up the spout again! (Tickle fingers up outside of child's legs.)'

PLENARY

Swap the objects around and ask child to choose again. When child is familiar with the rhymes ask a classmate to join in and encourage them to do the pausing and the actions with the child to encourage communication with other children.

53. More Please! *cont.*

CONSOLIDATION ACTIVITY

Extend the range of rhymes to which the child has the chance to respond by asking for more, for example 'Round and round the garden like a teddy bear (PAUSE and WAIT), one step (PAUSE and WAIT), two step (PAUSE and WAIT) and (PAUSE and WAIT) tickle you under there!'

54. What's the Weather?

Learning Objective

P4 pupils listen and respond to familiar rhymes and stories.

Additional Skills

Auditory: listening to a familiar story.

Communication: making a choice between two objects.

Social communication: waiting a turn as part of a group.

Tactile: experiencing different sensory experiences.

Resources

Piece of thick card/hand-held fan

Water spray

Torch/disco light

Shaving foam

White/grey piece of material

Tray/basket

MAIN

- Children sit in a semicircle in a small group.
- Adult has all the props in a tray/basket sitting at the front of the group.
- Adult models using the props and the weather they represent (let the whole group enjoy the sensory experience):
  » Thick card/handheld fan – (waft the card/fan around the group) 'It's windy!'
  » Water spray – (gently spray the group) 'It's raining!'
  » Torch/disco light – (hold above the group) 'It's sunny!'
  » Shaving foam – (spray a small amount in your hand and clap) 'It's snowing!'
  » White/grey piece of material – (gently place over each child) 'It's cloudy!'
- Now sing the song to the tune of 'Frère Jacques': 'What's the weather? What's the weather? I don't know, I don't know, (Child's name) can you tell me, (Child's name) can you tell me?' At this point present the chosen child with two of the props (or more, depending on the child) and encourage them to choose through eye gaze, gesture or verbalisation. When they have selected a prop, say, for example, 'It's snowing!', and clap the shaving foam onto the child.
- Say '(Child's name)'s turn has finished.' And repeat the song, choosing a different child for the next turn.

PLENARY

Encourage different members of the group to come to the front and do the role of the adult, helping to sing the song, choosing a child and using the prop.

54. What's the Weather? *cont.*

CONSOLIDATION ACTIVITY

Create other sensory rhymes and stories that engage the child in choice-making, for example a story where the child chooses an item of dressing up such as gloves/hat/scarf or a different smell using food flavouring.

55. Follow the Story

Learning Objective

P4 pupils show some understanding of how books work.

Additional Skills

Gross motor: jumping/stepping along the story.

Auditory: following instructions.

Visual: looking to see where to go next.

Resources

Sequential A3 laminated pages from familiar/class storybook

Original version of the book

Blu Tack

Chalk

MAIN

- In a clear space in the classroom look at each of the laminated A3 story pages with the child in the order in which they appear in the book.

- As you look at each page, Blu Tack it securely to the floor so it makes a long line going in page order from left to right.

- Next encourage the child to explore the story from left to right by, for example, jumping from page to page, big or fairy steps from page to page, hopping from page to page, etc. Each time the child lands on the page encourage them to look at it to explore the story.

- Once the child has explored the story from left to right through several different movements, sit back together on the floor and collect the story up again, working from left to right.

- Once the A3 story is complete, turn each page over to read through the story once more, looking at the writing from left to right and turning the pages together.

PLENARY

Find a quiet, comfortable space in the classroom and sit with the child to explore the original version of the book, looking at the writing from left to right and turning the pages together.

CONSOLIDATION ACTIVITY

On the playground floor use chalk to draw several boxes in a line. With the child write or draw different familiar and motivating words, for example their name, favourite toy, etc. Encourage the child to jump into each box from left to right, stopping and looking

55. Follow the Story *cont.*

at the word/drawing in each box. Encourage child to mark-make in each box from left to right and repeat jumping/stepping/hopping into each box and looking at the marks they made.

56. Which Way Around?

Learning Objective

P4 pupils show some understanding of how books work.

Additional Skills

Visual: noticing that a picture is the wrong way around.

Fine motor: turning pages and turning book right way around.

Attention: engaging with an activity for increasing periods of time.

Resources

A4 book that is made up of labelled photos (one per page) of child, classmates and motivating toys/objects; start with two pages per subject then build up as child's attention builds (e.g. two pages of child, two pages with photos of very familiar classmates/family members, two pages of photos of motivating toy/object – one clear and big photo per page labelled with child's name, classmate's name, etc.)

MAIN

- Find a quiet, comfortable space in the classroom or school (ideally the library or book corner).

- Introduce the book to the child: 'Look! It's (child's name)'s photo book!'

- Look at the book together. Draw attention to the words, encourage child to look at them from left to right and to turn the pages with you/independently.

- Once the book has been looked at adult says 'Uh oh!' and makes a show of the book turning upside down!

- Look at the book together again, this time making a show of trying to see the pictures the right way up, for example putting the book on the floor and moving around to see it properly, moving head around, etc.

- Model for the child how to turn the book around and support them to turn it around independently.

- Repeat for each page.

- When the child turns around the book the right way up for the motivating object/toy pages, give specific praise ('Great turning the book around, now it's the right way up!') and give the child the object to explore for a brief period of time.

PLENARY

Look at the large A3 laminated pages from familiar/class storybook. Put them on a non-carpeted floor and spin them around; watch as they spin. If they land upside down, model turning the pages the correct way up. Support the child to spin the pages and correctly place them the right way up.

56. Which Way Around? *cont.*

Motivating toys/objects that match the photos

A3 laminated pages from familiar/class storybook

CONSOLIDATION ACTIVITY

Whenever exploring books/photos/symbols with the child across the school day present them to the child upside down and give them the opportunity to turn it the correct way up. Give specific praise (as in the activity) when they do so. Continue to model for child turning visual material such as books, photos and name cards. the correct way up before turning the pages or reading/looking at the material.

57. Playground Hunt

Learning Objective

P5 pupils match objects to pictures and symbols.

Additional Skills

Gross motor: using the playground apparatus.

Kinaesthetic: moving around to match the symbols.

Social communication: working as part of a small group.

Resources

Symbols or pictures of playground equipment, for example slide, climbing frame and roundabout, velcroed onto a laminated piece of card (choosing board)

Matching symbols or pictures attached to playground equipment

Symbol or picture of something in the classroom, such as a chair

Matching symbol or picture attached to object in the classroom

One- or five-minute sand timer

MAIN

- Using minimal language explain to child that today we are going on a playground hunt! We are going to use symbols/pictures to find equipment to explore.

- Adult models choosing, for example, chair symbol from the choosing board and looking around to find it in the classroom; when they find it they run over and match the symbol then sit in the chair.

- Now go out into the playground and support child to choose a symbol/picture from the choosing board, run around playground and match the symbol/picture to the equipment.

- Encourage child to explore and play on the equipment for a short period of time (one or five minutes, using a timer if needed) and then finish and find the next piece of equipment.

PLENARY

Invite some other children to come out to the playground. Children take it in turns to choose a symbol then race to the chosen piece of equipment and match the symbol or picture.

CONSOLIDATION ACTIVITY

Across the day, support the child to match symbols to familiar objects; for example when collecting resources for a lesson give the child a symbol of what is needed such as pens, paintbrushes, etc. then they match the symbol to the object when they have found it for the lesson.

58. Fishing for Toys

Learning Objective

P5 pupils select a few words, symbols or pictures with which they are particularly familiar and derive some meaning from text, symbols or pictures presented in a way familiar to them.

Additional Skills

Fine motor: manipulating the 'fishing rod'.

Visual: matching the symbol/picture to objects.

Attention: increasing ability to stay at an activity for longer periods of time.

Communication: requesting a motivating object/toy.

Resources

Builder's tray

Words, symbols or pictures of motivating toys with paper clips attached

Motivating objects/toys to match the words/symbols/pictures

'Fishing rods' – sticks with string attached with a magnet attached to the bottom of the string

One- or five-minute timer

MAIN

- Scatter the words/symbols/pictures with the paper clips attached in the builder's tray.

- Adult models for the child using the fishing rod to catch a word/symbol/picture and exchange it for the chosen motivating object or toy.

- Encourage the child to use the fishing rod to catch a word/symbol/picture and then exchange it for their desired toy or object.

- Allow the child to explore their selected object or toy for a short period of time (using a one- or five-minute timer if necessary) then repeat the fishing activity.

PLENARY

Sit with the child away from the builder's tray. Lay out the words/symbols/pictures that match the objects/toys. Adult selects an object/toy and shows it to the child; the child then finds and selects the word/symbol/picture to give to the adult in exchange for the object/toy.

CONSOLIDATION ACTIVITY

Across the day, support child to select words/symbols/pictures of items/activities/objects that they want or need and exchange with the adult to receive the selected item/activity/object.

59. What's in the Book?

Learning Objective

P5 pupils show curiosity about content at a simple level.

Additional Skills

Attention: developing joint attention skills.

Social communication: taking turns and waiting as part of a small group.

Communication: expressing through gesture/symbol/ verbalisation an answer in response to a question.

Resources

Range of big and small jungle animals, for example big lion, small lion, big elephant, small elephant

Tray/basket

Laminated book: on each page is text that reads, for example, 'big lion', and a picture/ symbol that matches the text

MAIN

• Children sit in a small group on the carpet.

• Adult introduces each character in the book, taking them out of the tray/basket and lining them up for the children to see. Adult pulls out the big elephant and says 'Here is big elephant!' Adult places the big elephant next to previously placed small elephant.

• Adult holds up the book, places it on floor in front of the children and chants 'What's in the book (clap, clap)? What's in the book (clap, clap)? What's in the book (clap, clap)? Let's look and see!'

• Adult makes a show of flicking through the book then shows the children the page they have found, saying for example 'Big lion is in the book!'

• Adult then chooses a child from group to find the big lion and match it to the book picture.

• Repeat the activity choosing different children to come and take a turn.

PLENARY

Adult lines up all the animals from the book again. Choose a child and ask them to come and find an animal to put back in the tray/basket, for example 'Luke can you find the small elephant and put him in the basket? Bye small elephant!' Repeat until all the animals have been tidied away.

CONSOLIDATION ACTIVITY

Repeat this activity with different objects, for example different coloured balls/boats, different sized farm

59. What's In the Book? *cont.*

animals and different patterned socks. Ensure that objects that require a two-key-word understanding are used, so that the child has to find the correct item from a range of other possibilities. For example, if there is a blue ball there must also be a green ball among other items so that the child has to understand both the object and colour to select the correct object.

60. Feely Bag Finds

Learning Objective

P5 pupils match objects to pictures and symbols.

Additional Skills

Visual: recognising that an object matches picture/symbol.

Gross motor: physically matching the object to the symbol.

Tactile: feeling different textures.

Social communication: taking turns and waiting as part of a small group.

Resources

Feely bag – any kind of bag where the children can't see what is inside

Range of tactile objects, for example Koosh ball, water snake, glitter wand

Matching board of pictures or symbols for the tactile objects

MAIN

- Before starting the activity, place all the tactile objects into the feely bag.

- Children sit in a small group with the adult at the front.

- Adult places the matching board in front of the children.

- Adult sings to the tune of 'Jingle Bells': 'Feely bag, feely bag, what's inside the feely bag? Put your hand in, feel about, when you're ready pull something out!'

- Adult chooses a child who puts their hand in the feely bag, pulls out a tactile object and matches it to the matching board.

- Child then explores the object while their friends take a turn.

PLENARY

Adult counts down '5, 4, 3, 2, 1, toys have finished!' Adult then selects children one at a time to come and place tactile object back into the feely bag. Repeat the activity.

CONSOLIDATION ACTIVITY

In messy play activities such as the sand tray, hide pictures/symbols of things that you might typically find at that activity, for example spades, sieves and funnels. When child finds the picture/symbol encourage them to match it to the corresponding object.

61. C-A-T

Learning Objective

P6 pupils match letters and short words.

Additional Skills

Visual: recognising words and letters.

Attention: maintaining concentration until a task is complete.

Social communication: negotiating the space and demands of the task.

Fine motor: searching and locating for hidden objects using hands.

Resources

Large tray with shredded paper

Magnetic letters

Pictures with C–V–C words underneath (allow around four per person)

MAIN

- Prior to starting, hide all the letters in shredded paper in a large tray next to the table. On the table, place the picture cards face down.

- In a small group, adult to ask the children to all sit around the table. Adult explains that they are all going to turn a card over and then they need to go and find the letters in the tray to make the word.

- Adult says 'Ready, steady, go!' – all the children turn over their first card and begin playing the game. The game continues until there are no cards left.

PLENARY

As a group, go around the table and ask each child to say the letters and the word that it spells.

CONSOLIDATION ACTIVITY

This activity could be replicated in the sand or water tray and be used to support the phonics or whole word reading lessons that you are teaching. It could also be used to support the children to learn the high-frequency words.

62. Go and Seek

Learning Objective

P6 pupils match letters and short words.

Additional Skills

Visual: recognising and tracking letters.

Attention: maintaining concentration until a task is complete.

Social communication: negotiating spaces and resources with other children.

Kinaesthetic: searching high and low for letters.

Resources

Flashcards with C-V-C words and pictures

Individual letters of the C-V-C words laminated with Blu Tack on the back

MAIN

- Prior to the lesson, hide all of the letters in the playground.

- Ask the children to sit in a group. Show the children some flashcards with C-V-C words and ask them to sound out and say the word.

- Tell the children that today we are going on a treasure hunt.

- Each child has a board with their first word on, and you all go outside and start the hunt.

- As the children find each letter, stick these on the board to make a word.

- When the word is complete, ask the child to take another board.

PLENARY

Come back to the classroom and go around the group asking each child to say out loud the word that they found.

CONSOLIDATION ACTIVITY

Make a display with the children of the words and letters that you used in the game. Use Velcro or Blu Tack so that these can be taken down to play again if the children request it.

63. It Goes in My House

Learning Objective

P6 pupils select and recognise or read a small number of words or symbols linked to a familiar vocabulary.

Additional Skills

Visual: recognising words and images.

Attention: maintaining concentration until a task is complete.

Social communication: sharing with a group.

Resources

Outline of a house on A3 paper

A4 page with 'No' written at the top

Pictures of regular household items with the word underneath; cut out

Pictures of non-household items with the word underneath; cut out

Glue

MAIN

- Place a picture of the outline of a house on the table. Next to it place a piece of paper that has 'No' written at the top.

- Place a mixture of the pictures in a pile next to the A3 house picture.

- Ask the child to read or recognise the word.

- Would they like it in their house? If yes, stick it in a room. If not, stick on the 'No' sheet.

PLENARY

As a group, come together and share the pictures. Ask children what their favourite item is and write this on the board. Is it the same for all the children?

CONSOLIDATION ACTIVITY

Set up a dolls' house (or other toy building) and find real items that the children can explore placing in the house. Is there anything else that they would like to add? Have some craft materials available so the children can extend their play by making resources.

64. Say It, Sing It

Learning Objective

P6 pupils select and recognise a small number of words or symbols linked to familiar vocabulary.

Additional Skills

Visual: match item to word.

Attention: see a task through to the end.

Social communication: turn taking and waiting.

Kinaesthetic: seeking out objects in the room.

Resources

Bag of nursery rhyme props (sheep, bus, duck, frog, spider, etc.)

Individual cards with the song name and simple picture

MAIN

- Place the board with the song choices at the front of the class with the props for each song.

- Let the children know that they can each choose a song, but they are going to be placed around the class so that they have to go and find the one they want.

- One by one the children choose a prop for the song that they want, and then go to find the corresponding card and return this to the adult.

- The child is supported to type in the word of the song on the computer (e.g. YouTube).

- All sing together, and then it is another child's turn.

PLENARY

When the session has finished, each child to place their prop and song card back into the bag and say goodbye to the group.

CONSOLIDATION ACTIVITY

Place the props in the book corner with some nursery rhyme songbooks so that the children can choose a rhyme and the story at the same time.

65. It Comes Next

Learning Objective

P7 pupils predict elements of a narrative.

Additional Skills

Communication: answering a 'what next' question.

Social communication: waiting for a turn.

Mathematical: sequencing.

Resources

Familiar book (e.g. *Dear Zoo*, *The Very Hungry Caterpillar*, *The Little Red Hen*)

Props to go with the chosen story

MAIN

- Set up the book and all of the props before the children join the group.

- An adult reads the title and models good reading practice (follows word with fingers, looks for clues in the pictures).

- Read the first page of the book together.

- Ask a child in the group to come and choose a prop by asking 'What happens next?'

- Continue reading and asking different children to choose props and ask them questions about the story.

PLENARY

Give the children time to play with the props and the book with limited adult support. The adult should listen out for story-telling language.

CONSOLIDATION ACTIVITY

In the book corner, leave the book and props out for at least a week so that the children can become familiar with the story and the sequence.

66. I Can See, I Can Say

Learning Objective

P7 pupils distinguish between print or symbols and pictures in text.

Additional Skills

Fine motor: sticking.

Social communication: waiting for a turn.

Resources

Familiar book (e.g. *Dear Zoo*, *The Very Hungry Caterpillar*, *The Little Red Hen*)

Photocopied pictures from the story

Key words from the story

Large pieces of paper

Glue

MAIN

- Using the same familiar book that you chose for 'It Comes Next' (Lesson 65) lay out all the images and words on a table.

- Invite the children to come and read the book with the adult.

- Adult to model pointing to the picture in the book and then scanning the table for the matching picture. Use the single word 'same'.

- Adult to read the text of a page, and then return to a key character name, point at it and repeat it. Model scanning the table to find the same word. Match this and say 'same'.

- Support a child to go through the same process with identifying a picture and each person taking a turn.

- Repeat with each child searching for a word.

PLENARY

On a large piece of paper make a simple display with the pictures and the words. If they match, use them as labels. Allow the children time to explore the different pictures and text while this is happening. If a child is particularly interested in one image or text, then open the book and show them where it comes in the story.

CONSOLIDATION ACTIVITY

Make a display of environmental print and logos (e.g. supermarket shopping bag, front page of popular newspaper, food wrapping) so that the children can start understanding the difference between picture and text within their environment.

67. Read It Back

Learning Objective

P7 pupils show an interest in the activity of reading.

Additional Skills

Communication: retelling a story.

Social communication: working with a partner.

Auditory: listening to words and key refrains.

Fine motor: manipulating puppets.

Resources

A class story

Puppets and props from the story

Recordable microphone (or tablet that records voice, and a toy microphone)

MAIN

• Set up a quiet area of the class with either a recordable microphone or a toy microphone and a tablet that can record.

• Set up a familiar storybook to the child and a range of puppets and props that go with the story.

• The adult models reading the book and turning the pages, using the puppets to tell the story.

• Adult to turn on the microphone or tablet and ask the child to ask the puppets to read the story.

PLENARY

Sit together with the book and play the recording of the story.

CONSOLIDATION ACTIVITY

Encourage the child's classmates to join in telling stories with different puppets. Each child could have a different role, such as narrator, recorder and puppet master.

68. Take a Guess

Learning Objective

P7 pupils predict elements of a narrative.

Additional Skills

Communication: verbalising guesses.

Social communication: taking turns.

Auditory: listening to words and key refrains.

Resources

Big book to read to the class

Post-it sticky notes

MAIN

- Before the lesson, go through the book and place Post-it notes over any character word or familiar word to the children.

- Ask the children to gather around for big book story time.

- Read the first page, and act surprised that there is a word that is hidden; ask the children if anyone can guess the word.

- Let the children come and take the Post-it notes off the page, and read the sentence again, with everyone joining in the missing word.

PLENARY

Show the children the book that you are going to read tomorrow, but this time the title has been covered. Can anyone guess what the title might be?

CONSOLIDATION ACTIVITY

Cover up some words in some of the children's favourite books; if they come and show you, act surprised and ask them to help you work out the missing word.

69. The Letters in My Name

Learning Objective

P7 pupils know their name is made up of letters.

Additional Skills

Fine motor: searching and grasping letters.

Social communication: working as part of a small group.

Tactile: searching within materials.

Resources

Water tray/builder's tray

Magnetic letters

Shredded paper

Large pieces of paper

Pens

Name card for each child

MAIN

- Before the lesson, fill up a water tray or builder's tray with shredded paper and all the letters that you have collected.

- Once the children arrive, give them each a card with their name on it.

- Ask them to read their name.

- Then point to each of the letters and say the name of the letter (or the letter sound if you are teaching phonics).

- Model searching in the tray for something, then pull out a letter. Track it along the name and see if it matches.

- Support the children to do the same; initially they may need support but, as they get the hang of it, move away so that they can work for themselves.

- Once the children have found the letters of their name, they can swap boards and find a friend's name.

PLENARY

Once everyone has found at least two names, all come to a large table covered in paper and alphabet strips. Spend time mark-making or writing the letters.

CONSOLIDATION ACTIVITY

Wherever possible, ask the children to write the letters of their name on their work and say them out loud so that they begin making the connection between a familiar word and the letters within it.

70. The Treasure Chest

Learning Objective

P7 pupils show an interest in the activity of reading.

Additional Skills

Visual: recognising words and images.

Social communication: sharing with a group or adult.

Fine motor: manipulating items of clothing.

Resources

Eye patches

Strips of spotty fabric for bandannas

Cardboard box decorated to look like a treasure chest

Selection of pirate-themed books, placed in the box

Beanbags and cushions in book corner

MAIN

- Have beanbags and cushions set up in the book corner.

- Place all the dressing up clothes on the table. Give children time to choose and dress up, adults too.

- Bring the 'treasure chest' out of the cupboard; be very expressive with your voice and body actions. Treat it like something really special and precious.

- Place the box down slowly and ask the children to gather around.

- Open the box and, with excitement, choose a book; hold it like it is the best thing you have ever seen.

- Let the children one by one take a turn at choosing.

- Adults to spend time with the children reading together.

PLENARY

When the session has finished, ask the children to very carefully put their book back into the chest for another day. Give them time to take their role play clothes off.

CONSOLIDATION ACTIVITY

Theme your book corner and have books, puzzles, puppets and dressing up all linked with a theme. You could do the jungle, the seaside or a party, to suggest a few.

71. It Has Got Three in It

Learning Objective

P8 pupils associate sounds with patterns in rhymes, with syllables and with words or symbols.

Additional Skills

Kinaesthetic: using the instruments on different body parts.

Social communication: taking turns.

Auditory: listening to words and sounds.

Resources

Tray and blanket

Range of everyday objects (e.g. whistle, paper, sharpener, washing up liquid, water)

Instruments for each group member

MAIN

- Place the items on a tray in the middle of the circle and lay a cover over the top.

- Ask the children to all sit in a circle; give each child an instrument, except one.

- The child who has no instrument goes to the tray and chooses an item, and they tell the group what it is.

- The first time, the adult will model clapping the syllables of the word and asking the children to copy.

- Repeat this game until the children feel they can take turns to clap the syllables too.

PLENARY

As each child puts their instrument away, they say their name and use the instrument to sound out the syllables.

CONSOLIDATION ACTIVITY

In the book corner, put a tablet and headphones with a range of nursery rhymes that the children can access independently.

72. The Wind Blew Them Away

Learning Objective

P8 pupils understand that words, symbols and pictures convey meaning.

Additional Skills

Visual: scanning the environment.

Social communication: sharing with a group or adult.

Auditory: listening to instructions.

Resources

Pictures of your current topic

Words, or words and symbols, on labels that correspond to the pictures

Large pieces of paper

Glue

MAIN

• Prior to the lesson, place a range of pictures in different places either around the classroom or in the playground.

• Tell the children that we are going on a picture hunt, as the wind blew all the pictures away.

• Give each child a label that has the word (or word and symbol) of the picture they need to find.

• When they find the picture, encourage them to come to the table and stick the picture and the word in the class book.

• Give the child another word and repeat.

PLENARY

When all the pictures have been found and glued down, read together.

CONSOLIDATION ACTIVITY

At the art table, the children could have large pieces of paper to make a cover for their book. Then together hole-punch the pages and thread string through. Place the finished book in the reading corner.

73. Glitter Letters

Learning Objective

P8 pupils recognise at least half the letters of the alphabet by shape, name or sound.

Additional Skills

Visual: recognising whole letters from only part of the letter.

Social communication: listening to others and taking turns independently.

Fine motor: mark-making with glue and glitter.

Resources

Black paper

Glue in a bottle with a spout

Glitter

Tray

Whiteboard

Dry wipe whiteboard pen

MAIN

- Children sit in small group.

- At the front of the group, adult models using the glue to squeeze out part of, for example, the letter A, slowly saying 'Big line down, big line down, little line across.'

- As children recognise the letter being drawn encourage them to shout out the name of the letter.

- Adult models shaking glitter all over the glue letter then shaking the glitter off into the tray to reveal the letter they have written.

- Repeat for other letters.

- When the children are familiar with the activity, whoever was first to recognise the letter comes to the front to write their own glitter letter, and their friends have to guess what they are writing.

- Tidy away the activity when all the children have had a turn.

PLENARY

Adult holds up the whiteboard and pen. Adult starts to make the sound of the letter, for example 'a, a, a', and begins to write it. Whoever shouts out the name of the letter first comes to the front to take a turn. Repeat for other letters.

CONSOLIDATION ACTIVITY

In other activities such as the sand tray and flour tray, adult begins to write letters, encouraging child to recognise letters and then write them themselves.

74. Word Hunt

Learning Objective

P8 pupils can read a growing repertoire of familiar words or symbols including their own names.

Additional Skills

Tactile: experiencing different textures.

Fine motor: using a range of different tools that require different grips.

Visual: recognising familiar words.

Resources

Four trays

Range of sensory media: flour, cornflakes, lentils, etc.; work up the messy play hierarchy according to individual child, e.g. cornflour and water, jelly

Fine motor implement for picking up laminated words (large plastic tweezers, chopsticks, pegs, etc.)

Range of familiar and less familiar laminated words

Objects or pictures to match the words

Finish box

MAIN

- Adult to set up the four trays on a table with a different type of sensory media in each one.

- Place a selection of laminated words in each tray.

- Place matching objects/pictures on table in front or behind where the trays are set out.

- Model to the child hunting for a word in one of the trays using a fine motor tool, for example the tweezers.

- When adult finds a word, model matching it to the corresponding picture/object.

- Encourage the child to take part in the activity.

- When they are familiar with the activity ask the child to invite classmates to take part and race each other to see who can match the most words the quickest.

PLENARY

When it is time to tidy up adult counts down '5, 4, 3, 2, 1, it's time to finish.' Show the child the object and ask them to find the matching word before placing the object into the finish box.

CONSOLIDATION ACTIVITY

Across the day ask the child to match familiar words to objects or objects to familiar words. For example when gathering resources for an activity, write the word 'pencil' on a whiteboard and ask them to find the matching object; when finding a friend to work with write the name of the classmate on a whiteboard and ask the child to find their friend.

75. Snack Time Shopping

Learning Objective

P8 pupils understand that words, symbols and pictures convey meaning.

Additional Skills

Communication: asking another person for a required item.

Visual: recognising that words/symbols/pictures correspond to objects.

Kinaesthetic: walking to local/classroom shop.

Social communication: understanding conversation rules in local community.

Resources

Laminated words/symbols/pictures (according to child's individual level) of items to buy in the shop, at reception desk, in classroom or 'shop', for example bananas, apples and crackers with soft Velcro on the back

Choosing board

MAIN

- Explain to the child that we need to go shopping for food for snacks!

- On the choosing board line up the words/symbols/pictures of the options for snacks.

- Ask the child to choose two, three, four or more. snack items and place them on the laminated shopping list.

- Explain to the child that we are going to the 'shop' to buy the items on our shopping list.

- Walk to the shop and support the child to look at the words/symbols/pictures on their shopping list and find the corresponding items in the shop, adding them to the shopping basket.

- If possible use a dry wipe marker pen to tick off the items as you add them to the basket.

- When all the items have been found, encourage the child to take the shopping basket to the till and pay for the items.

PLENARY

At snack time or when returning from the shop ask the child to tell another adult or classmate what they have bought in the shop, referring to the words/symbols/pictures on their shopping list. If possible support the child to ask their classmates what they would like for snacks by using the words/symbols/pictures to show the child what snack item they would like.

CONSOLIDATION ACTIVITY

When items are needed for cooking lessons, messy play, etc. support the child to make a shopping list in the same way (or referring to the ingredients list) and use the shopping list to go and buy/collect the needed items.

75. Snack Time Shopping *cont.*

Laminated A4 card with 'Shopping List' written at the top then squares of hard Velcro underneath

Money (ideally real coins)

Dry wipe whiteboard pen

Teaching note: depending on the level of the child and the school's risk assessment policy, think about where the best place to 'shop' might be. If possible going out in the local community is most meaningful but going to the reception desk or kitchen might be another option if leaving the school is not possible.

76. Roll Me a Word

Learning Objective

P8 pupils understand that words, symbols or pictures convey meaning.

Additional Skills

Gross motor: throwing the big pocket dice.

Visual: recognising the word/symbol/picture matching an object.

Social communication: taking turns in a small group.

Attention: watching classmates take a turn.

Resources

Large pocket dice

At least six words/symbols/pictures of props from familiar/class story that fit into the pockets on the die

Matching props from story

Copy of the story

MAIN

- Children sit in a small group in a semicircle.
- Choose a child to come and roll the dice.
- Child rolls the dice; whichever word/symbol/picture is on the top they have to find the matching prop from the story.
- If possible encourage the child to look through the book to find the part of the story that matches the prop.
- Child chooses a classmate to be the next child to take a turn rolling the dice.
- Introduce new words and story props to the activity as the children become more familiar with the lesson and the story.

PLENARY

Support the group to retell the familiar story by lining up the words and the props in sequence along with the story.

CONSOLIDATION ACTIVITY

Place the pocket dice with the words/symbols/pictures in the book corner with the corresponding props, and encourage the children to explore the game and the story with their classmates, independent of adult support.

WRITING

77. My Car Drew It!

Learning Objective

P4 pupils make marks in their preferred mode of communication.

Additional Skills

Social interaction: collaborate and share resources with classmates.

Kinaesthetic: moving location around the paper.

Resources

Large pieces of paper

Felt-tip pens

Vehicles

Sellotape

MAIN

- Place a very large piece of paper on the floor. Stick pens to the back of the vehicles so that the tip of the pen will make marks on the paper.

- Invite the children to come and create a town with you.

- Encourage the children to share and swap the vehicles.

- Ask them about what they are drawing.

PLENARY

Ask each of the children to either write their name or find their name label and place it near to the marks that they have made.

CONSOLIDATION ACTIVITY

Once the children are used to mark-making on a large scale with adult support, this could be placed out as a continuous provision around the classroom so that the children return to it at points during the week.

78. Sticky Marks

Learning Objective

P4 pupils make marks or symbols in their preferred mode of communication.

Additional Skills

Tactile: touching wet and sticky mixture.

Gross motor: pouring and mixing.

Auditory: listening to instructions.

Resources

Aprons

Bowls

Spoons

Cornflour

Food colouring in a range of colours

Small jugs

Zip bags

A4 cards with marks (circle, squiggle, straight line, spiral, smiley face, etc.)

MAIN

• Have the ingredients to make the messy bags placed together on the table. Give each child an apron and have the visual instructions at the table.

• Ask the children to pour the cornflour into a bowl.

• The children then choose a food colour and add this to the jug of water.

• They pour half the water into the cornflour and mix. (You will need to play around with the amounts of flour and water that you use. The consistency should be gloopy.)

• Each child then works in a pair, either with an adult or another child, and spoons the mixture into a zip bag.

• Everyone helps to tidy up.

• The bags are stuck to a table while this happens.

• The adult shows the group a card with a mark on it (squiggle, circle, etc.) and all the children replicate this mark by running their finger over the outside of the bag. This will leave a mark in the cornflour mixture.

• Repeat.

PLENARY

Everyone helps tidy up any remaining bowls and puts away their equipment.

CONSOLIDATION ACTIVITY

Once the activity is finished, the bags can be taped to a window. This allows light to shine through and the children to make marks throughout the day. You can place some visuals in the same area to provide inspiration.

79. They Are Hiding

Learning Objective

P4 pupils make marks in their preferred mode of communication.

Additional Skills

Tactile: exploring dry materials.

Visual: noticing initial letters.

Resources

Builder's tray

Dry lentils

Laminated photos of each member of the class

Laminated name labels of each member of the class

MAIN

- Place all the photos in a builder's tray and cover it with dry lentils.

- Model to the children searching for a photo in the tray. When they find their own photo, ask them to look for their name label.

- Give them a chance to mark-make the first letter of their name.

- Ask them if they can find their friend.

PLENARY

At the end of the session, ask the children to help match the photos and names and place them in a bag for another day.

CONSOLIDATION ACTIVITY

Take the photos and labels outside. Hang up some string and leave pegs out. Can the children hang up the photos and find the correct label?

80. Wash It Off

Learning Objective

P4 pupils show that they understand that marks and symbols convey meaning.

Additional Skills

Social interaction: negotiating spaces with others.

Fine motor: manipulating different materials.

Visual: recognising familiar letters.

Resources

Chalk

Washing up brush per child

Washing up bowl with water

Aprons

MAIN

- On the playground, write in chalk everyone's name and the name of other people in the school that are known to the children. Write them multiple times and in a large font.

- Give each of the children a washing up brush and place a washing up bowl of water in the centre.

- With all the children in aprons, shout out a name and ask all the children to find it. Adults to model tracing around the words to rub the chalk from the playground.

- Repeat until all the chalk has been washed off.

PLENARY

Ask the children to find a word that they can see in water marks and ask them what it is. Can they find their own name?

CONSOLIDATION ACTIVITY

You could take a pocket dice out with different everyday words in each pocket and as the dice is rolled, the children find the matching word and rub it out with water.

81. Who Is Here Today?

Learning Objective

P4 pupils show that they understand that marks and symbols convey meaning.

Additional Skills

Visual: noticing who is in the class that day.

Fine motor: manipulating different materials.

Attention: completing a task.

Resources

Magnetic board and magnets

Laminated photos of each member of the class

Laminated name labels of each member of the class

MAIN

- Place on a table all the photos of all the children and adults in the class. Place a magnetic board with magnets near to this. Place all the labels in a basket.

- Model to the children finding a picture and the correct name and placing it on the board. Each child to find their own picture and name and place it on the board.

- Then let the children know that this will be up each day, and that one child will be chosen to take the 'register' and place the people that are in the class today on the board.

PLENARY

Keep this up for a few weeks; ask a different child to take the morning and afternoon register. Ask another child to take it down at the end of the day.

CONSOLIDATION ACTIVITY

As the children get more experienced with this, place a weekly register sheet on a clipboard next to the board with a pencil attached to the clipboard with string. Ask the children to make tally marks to keep a formal register.

82. Mirror Image

Learning Objective

P5 pupils produce meaningful marks or symbols associated with their own name or familiar images.

Additional Skills

Fine motor: grasping a mark-making tool.

Visual: recognising own image.

Hand–eye co-ordination: co-ordinating looking at image and using mark-making tool.

Tactile: tolerating the feeling of face paint.

Resources

Acrylic/child safe mirror

Dry wipe marker pen in a range of colours

Laminated colour symbols to match the colours of the pens

Range of dressing up hats

Range of face paints

Blank face templates

MAIN

- At the table, adult models for the child looking in the mirror and recognising themselves.

- Support the child to do the same.

- Adult and child then draw features on the blank face templates (if the child scribbles, this is fine; adult models putting in eyes, mouth, nose, etc.).

- Look in the mirror again and this time use the dry wipe marker pen to mark on eyes, nose, mouth, etc. on the mirror.

- Now experiment dressing up using the different hats and face paints.

- Each time something is changed about the child's appearance, support them to mark this on the mirror using the dry wipe marker pen.

- When the child has finished dressing up, support them to write their name on the mirror using the dry wipe marker pen. Again scribble writing is fine; adult models how to write their name using letters.

PLENARY

Together take a picture of the child and then of their mirror image. Print out the photos and child mark-makes on the photos.

CONSOLIDATION ACTIVITY

When the child produces a piece of work such as artwork, ask them to write their name on their work. Again if they scribble-write, this is fine; adult to model writing their name using letters.

83. Family Tree

Learning Objective

P5 pupils produce meaningful marks or symbols associated with their own name or familiar images or events.

Additional Skills

Fine motor: cutting and sticking skills, using mark-making tools.

Visual: recognising familiar people in photos.

Attention: attending to and completing an activity for up to ten minutes.

Social communication: showing their work to their classmates.

Resources

Photocopies of photos of familiar family members

Glue sticks

Scissors appropriate to child's handgrip, for example left-handed scissors or long loop easy-grip scissors

Tree with branches drawn on a large piece of paper as a template

Range of coloured pens

MAIN

- Explain to the child that today we are going to make a family tree to show who is in our family.

- At the table look at the pictures of the child's family together and support the child to name who is in the photos using speech/symbols/gesture.

- Ask the child to choose a photo and support them as needed to cut the photo out of the page and then stick it onto the drawn tree.

- Repeat this with all the photos.

- Once the child has stuck all the photos on the tree ask them, for example 'Where's Mummy?' and encourage them to indicate the photo of their mum. Model writing 'Mummy' next to this photo and then encourage them to label the photo using one of the coloured pens.

- Repeat this for all the photos on the tree until the child has labelled all the photos.

PLENARY

Stand back and look at the child's tree with one or two classmates. Encourage the classmates to ask the child questions about who is in the photos and support the child to respond. Support the child to write their name on their work.

CONSOLIDATION ACTIVITY

Repeat this activity but with other photos and templates, for example a classroom template and pictures of classmates, and a 'likes' and 'dislikes' template and pictures of familiar food, etc.

Teaching note: when planning this lesson be sensitive to children's individual family situation and adapt as necessary; making a class tree might be a good alternative.

84. Splatter Mark-Making

Learning Objective

P5 pupils can trace, overwrite or copy shapes and straight-line patterns.

Additional Skills

Gross motor: accurately throwing material.

Fine motor: using finger or paintbrush to mark-make.

Tactile: engaging in messy play.

Social communication: turn taking as part of a pair.

Resources

J Cloths cut into four

Range of paint colours

Laminated colour symbols that match the paint colours velcroed onto a choosing board

Flat trays/transparent paint pots

White shower curtain (or large piece of paper taped to a table)

Paintbrushes (if child does not enjoy the experience of putting hands in paint)

MAIN

- Set up the activity by placing the shower curtain flat on the floor. Squeeze the paint colours onto flat trays so they can be clearly seen by the children. Place several bits of the J Cloth next to each paint tray.

- Bring the children over to the activity and ask them to sit next to the shower curtain.

- Adult models choosing paint colour symbol from the choosing board and then finding the matching colour paint.

- Adult places the piece of J Cloth into the paint and then throws the J Cloth onto the shower curtain to make a splat!

- Adult models using their finger to draw a straight line or a shape in the splatted paint.

- Adult then offers the paint choosing board to one of the children and the children take it in turns to take part in the activity.

PLENARY

Adult models taking a piece of A3 paper and laying it over one of the shapes in the paint splatter to create the shape on the paper. Hold it up for the children to see the copy of the shape on the paper. Adult then uses the chalk to colour in the shape created on the paper. The children follow the same method, using the paper to imprint the shapes and the chalk to colour in the shapes on the paper. Support the child to select their favourite to go up on the wall or to take home.

84. Splatter Mark-Making *cont.*

A3 pieces of white paper
(or coloured sugar paper)

Different coloured chalk

CONSOLIDATION ACTIVITY

During activities such as messy play in media such as flour, oats, shaving foam, etc. adult models using a finger to create pre-writing shapes such as straight lines, circles, swirls and waves, and supports the child to copy the marks made in the sensory media.

Teaching note: if you are able to this activity is great fun to do on the window!

85. Race Track

Learning Objective

P5 pupils can trace, overwrite or copy shapes and straight-line patterns.

Additional Skills

Attention: watching and imitating another person's actions.

Fine motor: using a pen grip to mark-make, manipulating small world objects.

Resources

Several sheets of white A3 paper

Masking tape

Pencil

Black marker pen

Laminated symbols of tree, person and stop sign velcroed to a choosing board

Small world cars

Range of paint colours

Flat trays

Laminated colour symbols to match the colours of the paints

Big chalk

MAIN

- Set up the activity by securely fastening the sheets of A3 white paper to the floor to form a large square or rectangle.

- Using the pencil, draw out a road that consists of straight lines, curves, loops, etc. and the straight lines down the middle of the 'road' in imitation of a race track.

- Use the black marker pen to trace over some of the pencil marks at different points in the track.

- Squeeze the paints into the flat trays and place the small world cars next to the tray.

- When the activity is set up bring over the child and explain that we are making a race track!

- Encourage the child to use the black marker pen to trace over the pencil marks to create the road.

- When this is done model choosing a colour symbol from the choosing board, finding that colour, selecting a small world car, placing the car in the paint and then placing the car at the start point on the track.

- Support the child to do the same.

- Now have a race around the track that has been created with the small world cars, creating paint marks as you go!

PLENARY

Show the child the choosing board with the laminated symbols of 'tree', 'person' and 'stop sign'. Encourage them to choose a symbol and exchange it with the adult. Adult then uses the pencil to draw the chosen item around the edge of the race track (using straight lines and shapes). The child traces over the shape with the black marker pen.

85. Race Track *cont.*

CONSOLIDATION ACTIVITY

Take the big chalk outside onto the playground and encourage the child to draw their own race track on the ground. Support the child to choose a classmate to come and race them around their created race track.

86. What Letter Can You See?

Learning Objective

P6 pupils copy letter forms.

Additional Skills

Fine motor: using a grip to mark-make using a mark-making tool.

Visual: finding and matching letters.

Auditory: following an instruction.

Resources

Large laminated letters A–Z (two copies)

Dry wipe marker pens

Big chalk

MAIN

- With the child lay out one set of the laminated alphabet letters on the table or the carpet, naming the letters as you go.

- Sing the song (to the tune of the ABC song) 'A, B, C, D, E, F, G, what letter can you see?'

- Adult then holds up a letter from the second set of laminated alphabet letters.

- Encourage the child to find the matching letter and then use the dry wipe marker pen to overwrite the letter.

- Play again and choose another letter to show the child.

- Play until the child has overwritten all the letters.

PLENARY

Sing the whole of the ABC song together. Encourage the child to mark-make on each letter as you sing its name.

CONSOLIDATION ACTIVITY

Take some big chalk outside to the playground. Adult draws large letters on the playground floor. With the child sing the song from the activity; encourage the child to find the letter the adult names and then use the chalk to overwrite the letter on the playground floor.

Teaching note: the child might scribble-write on the laminated letters; adult can model on their set of letters how to accurately overwrite the letters.

87. Fish for Your Name

Learning Objective

P6 pupils produce or write their name in letters or symbols.

Additional Skills

Fine motor: manipulating small objects.

Visual: recognising and matching letter symbols.

Attention: maintaining focus and attention to an activity for up to 10–15 minutes.

Resources

'Fishing rods' – sticks with string attached with a magnet attached to the bottom of the string

Paper clips

A5 laminated letters A–Z

Pegs

Clear written copy of the child's name

Builder's tray

Water

MAIN

- Attach the paper clips to the laminated letter symbols. Place the letter symbols in the builder's tray and cover with water (or blue tissue paper if you want this to be a dry activity). Next or near to the builder's tray make a washing line with the string and peg up the copy of the child's name.

- Encourage the child to come over to the activity. Model using the fishing rod to catch a letter, and hold it up to the copy of the child's name; if the letter is in the name, peg it up on the washing line, if not throw it back in the builder's tray.

- Support the child to do the same, fishing for all the letters in their name and then pegging them up on the washing line.

PLENARY

Once the child has found all the letters in their name support them to place them in the correct order to spell their name. Give specific praise to the child for spelling their name using letter symbols.

CONSOLIDATION ACTIVITY

Play the fishing game with other words the child might be learning to understand or spell such as C–V–C words. Encourage other children to come and play so that they can model for the child as well as support turn taking and social communication.

88. Light It Up

Learning Objective

P6 pupils produce or write their name in letters or symbols.

Additional Skills

Social interaction: waiting for the item needed.

Fine motor: manipulating objects.

Resources

Light box (or large see-through plastic box with lid) and string of fairy lights

Coloured plastic shot glasses with all alphabet letters on the base of the glass

Permanent marker pen

Laminated name card for each child

MAIN

• Set up the light box on a table that has space for children to move around.

• Give the box of coloured shot glasses to the children and ask them to set them out.

• Give each child their name card.

• Ask them to find the letters to spell their name.

• Once they have done this, take away the name cards and see if they can repeat.

• Can they spell their friend's name?

PLENARY

As the shot glasses go back into the box, everyone to say the letter of the alphabet. Adult models trying to spell some simple words as they go, and see if the children can say the whole word.

CONSOLIDATION ACTIVITY

Lots of activities can be done on the light box. Place name cards on the light box and a pack of beads. Let the children spend time placing these over the letters of their name.

89. Rub It Out Faster

Learning Objective

P6 pupils produce or write their name in letters or symbols.

Additional Skills

Social interaction: working with others.

Attention: increasing attention to ten minutes.

Auditory: following instructions.

Resources

Chalk

Timer

MAIN

- Out on the playground, half the group have a piece of chalk, and the other half of the group have a washing up brush.

- When the adult says 'Ready, steady, go!' the children have two minutes to either write their name in chalk, or rub out their name with water. Adults to support where needed.

- When the timer runs out, the adult shouts, 'Stop!' The writing team count how many they have left and put this on the tally. The tally can be in chalk in a separate area so it is not washed away.

- The children then swap sides.

- Carry on playing this for a few rounds so that the children can become independent.

PLENARY

Everyone go to the tally board and count the marks to see which team won!

CONSOLIDATION ACTIVITY

Once taught in the structured lesson, this activity can be placed out at playtime so that the children can play with other children.

90. Who? What? Where?

Learning Objective

P6 pupils produce or write their name in letters or symbols.

Additional Skills

Social communication: answering questions appropriately.

Attention: increasing attention to ten minutes.

Visual: noticing what is happening in pictures.

Resources

Printout of photos

Strips of card

Pencils

Whiteboards and pens

Display board and pins

MAIN

- The next time a trip is planned, take photos of the children at key points through the day. Let them know that these photos will be used back in class.

- Have all the printed photos, large strips of card, whiteboards, and pens and pencils on the table.

- Adult to show the children the first picture. Ask the children, 'Who?' Wait for their response and then model writing this on the whiteboard. Then ask the children either 'What?' or 'Where?' Again, model writing this answer on the board. The simple sentence should read something like 'Abdul with giraffe'.

- Show the children the second picture and repeat the process. This time ask them to write their answers on their whiteboard.

- Ask each child to choose their favourite picture from the pile; spend time with each child composing a sentence on the whiteboard; and then give them the card and paper to write their label.

PLENARY

When everyone has finished, pin these to the display board with each of the pictures.

CONSOLIDATION ACTIVITY

Next time you have some class photos, print these out and leave them on the writing table with the same resources and key words so that the children can practise writing labels.

91. Alien Bob

Learning Objective

P7 pupils are aware of the sequence of letters, symbols and words.

Additional Skills

Communication: exploring language and sounds.

Attention: increasing attention to ten minutes.

Auditory: following instructions.

Resources

Paper

Coloured pencils

Laminating pouches and laminator

Grids (see Main)

Laminated letters to fit in grid

Strips of paper

Pencils

MAIN

• Ask each of the children in the group to draw an alien. Have plenty of visuals of aliens on the table to give the children ideas. Use prompts such as 'How many eyes does it have?' and 'What colour is it?'

• When each child has finished, laminate all of their aliens.

• Place the aliens on a table and place grids next to each alien; this is to indicate how long its name will be, for example four rectangles across or three rectangles across.

• Place a basket of cut-out laminated letters, each the same size as the rectangles in the grid, next to the aliens.

• Ask the children to find letters and make up a name for their alien. The adults will need to model this.

• If the children choose familiar names, adults to also model making up nonsense names to encourage the children to use their phonetic knowledge to sound out the word.

PLENARY

Once each alien has a name, the children write out their favourite names on card strips. These can be used as suggestions for the next time the activity is carried out.

CONSOLIDATION ACTIVITY

This would make a good display; place Velcro on the grids and letters and allow the children to play around with the sequence of letters and words.

92. Say It, Spell It, Write It

Learning Objective

P7 pupils are aware of the sequence of letters, symbols and words.

Additional Skills

Communication: exploring language and sounds.

Attention: increasing attention to ten minutes.

Auditory: following instructions.

Fine motor: searching for letters.

Resources

A4 writing frame split into three sections' ('say it', 'spell it', 'write it') and laminated

Basket of magnetic letters

Whiteboard pens

Basket of pictures or objects with labels of familiar items (cats, cars, trains, people, etc.)

MAIN

- Place a basket of pictures (or objects) in the middle of the table. Give each child a writing frame and a pen.

- Adult to model taking an item from the basket, placing it in the 'say it' section and saying the name, for example 'cat'.

- The adult models searching in the basket of magnetic letters for the letters to spell 'cat' and places these in the 'spell it' section.

- The adult then models writing the word 'cat' in the 'write it' section.

- Each child to choose an item from the basket and repeat the process that the adult went through.

- Start the ten-minute timer and see how many pictures/objects the children can work through.

PLENARY

As the timer runs out, go around the group and ask each child to say it, spell it and show their writing for the last item that they chose.

CONSOLIDATION ACTIVITY

Change the items in the basket to key story or topic vocabulary so that the children begin to build a repertoire of words to use in their play and work.

93. Sensory Poetry

Learning Objective

P7 pupils group letters and leave spaces between them as though they are writing separate words.

Additional Skills

Communication: exploring language and sounds.

Attention: increasing attention to ten minutes.

Auditory: following instructions.

Visual: looking at resources to support writing.

Resources

A4 themed writing frame based on current topic with sentence starters 'I see', 'I hear', 'I taste', 'I smell' etc. on different lines

Visuals of 'I see', 'I hear', 'I taste', 'I touch', etc.

Pencils

Word bank visual

Whiteboard and pens

MAIN

- Read the topic book to the children – weather or seasons works well for this lesson.

- Show the children a set of visuals for the senses ('I hear', 'I see', etc.)

- Adult to model placing one visual down and forming a sentence, for example 'I hear wind'. The adult then repeats this with another sense talking to the children about the senses.

- Let the children take a turn with choosing senses and creating short sentences. Adult to model using the word bank for ideas.

- After a few times at trying, present the children with their writing frame for the poem. Encourage them to look at the sentences they have completed with the visuals to support them.

- Adults to ensure good pencil grip.

PLENARY

When the group have finished, come together in a circle and each child presents their poem to the group.

CONSOLIDATION ACTIVITY

This could also be done as an acrostic poem with the name of the child forming the sentence starters to make this more challenging.

94. The Dice Makes a Sentence

Learning Objective

P7 pupils group letters and leave spaces between them as though they are writing separate words.

Additional Skills

Social communication: working with others.

Attention: increasing attention to ten minutes.

Auditory: following instructions.

Visual: looking at pictures and words.

Resources

Three large pocket dice

One dice with character pictures and labels (e.g. old lady, dragon, pilot)

One dice with action pictures and labels (jumped high, ate pizza, sang loudly, etc.)

One dice with location pictures and labels (e.g. under water, on the bus, by the sea)

Large pieces of paper

Pens

MAIN

- Place each of the three pocket dice on the floor on top of a large piece of paper.

- Ask a child to come and roll each of the dice and then line them up.

- Adult to model reading the sentence, for example 'The girl ate pizza on the bus.'

- Adult to write this sentence on the paper.

- Another child takes a turn to roll the dice and they read the sentence. Support the child to 'write' their sentence, encouraging them to form as many letters recognisably as possible.

- Repeat with the group.

PLENARY

After everyone has taken a turn, read some of the sentences; some should be funny!

CONSOLIDATION ACTIVITY

You can add more dice to include other sentence components such as time of the day, days of the week, etc.

95. The Office Needs You!

Learning Objective

P7 pupils group letters and leave spaces between them as though they are writing separate words.

Additional Skills

Social communication: working with others.

Attention: increasing attention to ten minutes.

Auditory: following instructions.

Visual: looking at resources to support writing.

Resources

Box of office supplies (folders, letters, pens, paper, tape, stickers, etc.)

Pretend email from the receptionist

MAIN

- Tell the children that the school receptionist has become very busy and needs their help.

- Show the children the box of filing, envelopes, folders, labels and all the other resources that you have found, and ask the children if they can help.

- Together, choose part of the classroom that can be set up as the role play, and allow the children to set this up with adults modelling and supporting, not taking the lead.

- Show the children an email that you have 'received', saying that the receptionist needs a leaflet to send home about an event next week and can the children create it?

PLENARY

After the session, make the role play area tidy and ready for more play.

CONSOLIDATION ACTIVITY

Each session, present the children with a different task that needs to be carried out in order to support the receptionist.

96. Come for a Party!

Learning Objective

P8 pupils show an awareness that writing can have a range of purposes.

Additional Skills

Social communication: communicating an idea to another person.

Fine motor: handling and manipulating writing tools.

Gross motor: walking appropriately in the local community.

Resources

Paper

Pens

Envelopes

Stamps

Craft materials

Example party invites

Clear invite template with spaces to write the name of the person invited, what they are invited to, the time and date and who the invite is from

MAIN

• Before this lesson arrange a time and date to invite parents and carers to come for a tea party with their children. Inform the parents and/or carers that their children will be sending invites home.

• Children sit in a semicircle on the carpet. Ask the children 'Who has been to a party before?' and talk about what happens at a party. Then show the children an example party invite and explain that how they know they are invited to a party is that they get an invite.

• Describe what is in an invite, for example the name of the person invited, what they are invited to, the time and date and who the invite is from.

• Adult explains that the class is going to have a party for their mums, dads or other carers and they need to make an invite for them!

• Support the child to complete their invite template, by copying writing, selecting and using symbols or independent writing.

• Encourage the children to decorate the invite to make them look really appealing.

PLENARY

When the invite is completed bring the children back to the semicircle. Explain that we need to send the invites to the person we have invited! Adult models placing an invite into an envelope, writing the address on the envelope and sticking on the stamp. Support all the children to do this with their envelopes (adults to write addresses on envelopes, support child to write, for example 'Mummy', and if able). Walk together to the post box to post the invites home. Ask the parents to let you know when the invites arrive so you can talk about it with the child.

96. Come for a Party! *cont.*

CONSOLIDATION ACTIVITY

Ask the parents and/or carers to bring along their invites to the party to support the child to understand that writing an invite meant that the person could come to the party. Have a tea party together and celebrate!

To consolidate the use of invites, or if inviting parents and/or carers to school is not possible, host a class party and make invites for friends in different classes. Another possibility is to host a teddy tea party and write invites for the different teddies or toys in the classroom.

Teaching note: if the child is using symbols to create sentences rather than writing, prepare the symbols needed to complete the invite template beforehand. If possible add an element of scissor work to support pre-writing skills, for example cutting out the symbol they need for the sentence.

97. Wish You Were Here...?

Learning Objective

P8 pupils show an awareness that writing can have a range of purposes.

Additional Skills

Communication: commenting on a past event.

Social communication: communicating an idea to another person.

Fine motor: handling and manipulating writing tools.

Resources

Photos of a recent trip or event

Postcard template

Examples of postcards

Glue sticks

Scissors appropriate to child's handgrip, for example left-handed scissors or long loop easy-grip scissors

Stamps

Pens/pencils

Interactive whiteboard (or another way of displaying photos digitally)

MAIN

- Before this lesson take photos of the child on a class trip or taking part in an exciting school event, for example going to the park/zoo/farm/shop or science/ world book day, etc. Print these photos out (ideally four to a page).

- In a small group look at the photos from the recent trip/event on the interactive whiteboard and encourage the children to comment on what they did, what they can see, what they liked/disliked, etc.

- Then explain that it would be great to tell the people at home all about the trip/event, and that one way people share what they have done in different places is by writing a postcard to people who weren't there. Discuss who wasn't on the trip/event, for example Mummy, Daddy, sister, brother, Gran.

- Look at example postcards.

- Explain that today the children are going to make their own postcards to send to someone who wasn't on the trip/event to tell them about what they did.

- At the table support the child to choose their favourite photo from the trip/event, cut out the photo and stick it to the front of the postcard.

- On the back of the postcard support the child to copy writing, select and use symbols or independently write a short sentence based on their comments about the photos, for example 'I like the zoo.'

- Support the child to write their name at the bottom of the postcard.

- Ask the child who they would like to send it to and then to write/copy/use a symbol of that person at the top of the address line.

- Adult then models good writing practice by writing the address of the person.

- Support the child to stick on the stamp.

97. Wish You Were Here...? *cont.*

PLENARY

Come back to the semicircle and encourage the children to share their postcards with each other. Walk to the local post box and post the postcards! Ask whoever the postcard was sent to, to let you know when it arrives so that you can talk about how writing can be used to tell people what happens in their day.

CONSOLIDATION ACTIVITY

When it is the weekend or the holidays, send the children home with some blank postcard templates and ask the parents and/or carers to encourage the child to write postcards that can be shared with classmates when they come back to school. The children can draw on the front of the postcard if they don't have access to printed photos.

98. Word Mix Up

Learning Objective

P8 pupils show an understanding of how text is arranged on a page.

Additional Skills

Fine motor: using a pincer grip to pick up small items.

Communication: making a short sentence.

Social communication: taking turns as part of small group.

Resources

Two laminated short sentence strips (can be words or symbols depending on child's understanding), for example 'I see cat', 'The boy is happy' and 'Today is Monday'

Two laminated individual words to match the words in the sentence

Paper clips

Builder's tray

'Fishing rods' – sticks with string attached with a magnet attached to the bottom of the string

MAIN

- Attach the paper clips to the laminated individual words. Put all the individual words mixed up into the builder's tray. Place one copy of the laminated sentence strips either side of the builder's tray.

- Support the child to choose a friend to play the game with.

- Child A stands one side of the builder's tray, Child B the other.

- Explain that the first to complete all the sentences is the winner! However, the children have to find the words in the same order as the sentence.

- The children take turns to use the fishing rod to find a word and match it to the sentence to build the sentence from left to right.

PLENARY

Once the children have made all the sentences, support them to read the sentences, pointing at each word and working from left to right.

CONSOLIDATION ACTIVITY

Once the child understands the game, start extending the sentences and invite more children to play. Also, in writing lessons remind the child of the game to support them to write from left to right.

Teaching note: it might be useful to play this game with the child individually before introducing a classmate/small group. Also, start off with just one or two sentences and then build up to more as the child gets more familiar with the game.

99. Pair Up

Learning Objective

P8 pupils can show an understanding of how text is arranged on a page.

Additional Skills

Social communication: waiting and taking turns appropriately as part of a group.

Visual: recognising the way text should be arranged on a page or in a sentence.

Communication: discussing an activity with a classmate.

Resources

Two sets of laminated A5 cards that show text arranged correctly or incorrectly on a page or in a sentence, for example two cards with all the writing in a vertical line, two cards with sentences going from left to right, two cards with words jumbled over the page, etc.

Two A3 pieces of paper with 'Yes' and 'No' written on them

MAIN

• Set up the activity by shuffling the cards and laying them out at random on the table top.

• Support the child to choose a friend to come and play the game.

• The children take it in turns to turn two cards over and try to find a match.

• When they find a match, place the pair to one side and keep trying.

• Once all the pairs have been found look at the cards together.

• Sort them onto the 'Yes' and 'No' pieces of paper according to whether the text is correctly arranged on the page or in a sentence.

• Encourage the children to discuss and negotiate with each other as they decide which page they should sort the cards onto.

PLENARY

Once all the cards have been sorted ask the children to choose their favourite from the 'Yes' page and then use messy media or dry wipe pens and whiteboards to copy how the text is arranged.

CONSOLIDATION ACTIVITY

When looking at books or other pieces of writing with the child, comment on how the text is arranged, for example from left to right and on different lines, to support the learning of language related to text arrangement.

100. Stop! Go!

Learning Objective

P8 pupils show an awareness that writing can have a range of purposes.

Additional Skills

Social communication: communicating with classmates in a small group.

Communication: giving and responding to instructions.

Fine motor: using an appropriate pencil grip to write a word or letter.

Resources

Whiteboard

Dry wipe marker pen

Laminated 'Stop' and 'Go' symbols

Laminated action symbols, for example jump, hop, run, clap

MAIN

- In the hall or the playground ask the children to stand in a semicircle.

- Choose a child to come to the front of the group and support them to write 'Stop' on one side of the whiteboard and 'Go' the other side.

- Ask the child to choose an action symbol, show it to their classmates and then use their 'Go' writing to get the group to start the action!

- Encourage the child to use their 'Stop' symbol to stop the action. Choose another action and go again.

- Count down '5, 4, 3, 2, 1, (child's name)'s turn has finished' and choose another child to come to the front.

- Encourage the children to only use the written symbols to communicate the action and when to stop and when to go.

PLENARY

Once all the children have had a turn using their writing/symbols to instruct the group, ask them to stand back in a semicircle. Now the adult uses the pen and whiteboard to draw different action symbols and the children complete the action – again using no words, only writing and symbols. Adult then writes instructions for the next part of the lesson, for example 'Line up' and 'Walk back to class'.

CONSOLIDATION ACTIVITY

With the child make signs for other routines/games and use these in small groups to communicate using written words or symbols across the day.

Teaching note: if the child finds writing difficult they can mark-make on the laminated symbols and use those instead of the whiteboard.

101. Roll Call

Learning Objective

P8 pupils can write or use their preferred mode of communication to set down their names with appropriate use of upper- and lower-case letters or suitable symbols.

Additional Skills

Gross motor: throwing the pocket dice.

Fine motor: using mark-making tools to write their name.

Attention: maintaining focus and attention for length of the activity.

Resources

Two large pocket dice

Laminated letters of child's name with appropriate upper- and lower-case letters

Large laminated copy of the child's name using appropriate upper- and lower-case letters

Dry wipe marker pen

MAIN

- Set up the activity by placing the laminated letters of the child's name in the pockets of the pocket dice. Place the large laminated copy of the child's name near where the activity will take place.

- Show the child the activity. Say that today we are going to make names using upper-case (show an upper-case letter) and lower-case letters (show a lower-case letter).

- The child rolls the pocket dice to first find the upper-case letter of their name and then the other letters of their name. As they find each letter, support the child to remove it from the pocket and match to the large laminated copy of the child's name.

- Reinforce the language 'upper'- and 'lower'-case letters.

PLENARY

Once the child has found all the upper- and lower-case letters for their name, support them to overwrite the letters using the dry wipe pen. Once the child is confident doing this, encourage them to write their name using upper- and lower-case letters without overwriting the laminated letters.

CONSOLIDATION ACTIVITY

Whenever looking at books or sentences point out the upper- and lower-case letters to the child. Once they are more confident making their name, repeat this activity using other names and words with a mix of upper- and lower-case letters, for example 'Mr Tumble'.

Kate Bradley had a background in occupational therapy before re-training as a teacher. She has worked in both mainstream and special needs schools, making lessons fun and engaging for SEN learners. Kate holds a Masters in Special and Inclusive Education, and lives in London.

Claire Brewer has been teaching pupils with severe learning difficulties, profound and multiple learning difficulties and autism since completing her PGCE at Goldsmiths University. Claire holds a Masters in Special and Inclusive Education, and lives in London.